All That I Am

Hearing the Voice of the Father

By Dianne Tylski

Copyright 2025
All That I Am
Hearing the Voice of the Father
Dianne Tylski
©2026
Printed in USA

ISBN Paperback: 9798278138990
ISBN Hardback: 9798278139270

All rights reserved.
This book is protected under the copyright laws of the United States of America. Any reproduction or unauthorized use of the material or artwork contained herein is prohibited without the express written permission of Dianne Tylski.
No part of this publication may be reproduced or transmitted in any form or by any means, electronic or mechanical, without permission in writing from the author.
Request for permission to make copies of any part of this work should be directed to
Dianne Tylski.

Editor: Brae Wyckoff

Cover art by: Get Covers (art design created by Dianne Tylski)

Scripture taken from the New King James Version.
Copyright © 1982 by Thomas Nelson.
Used by permission. All rights reserved.

Dedication

I dedicate this book to my late husband, Rich Tylski,
and my precious friend and prayer partner, Daryl Franz.
Your love and care walked me through some of the fiercest fires of my life.

Acknowledgments

My heartfelt thanks to Jill and Brae Wyckoff. Your leadership, passion, and devotion to bringing God into the arts have shaped and strengthened my own journey. I am truly grateful.

Contents

Dedication iii
Acknowledgments v
Introduction 1
January 4
February 36
March 66
April 98
May 130
June 162
July 194
August 226
September 258
October 290
November 322
December 354
Closing 387
About the Author 389

INTRODUCTION
All That I Am- Hearing the Voice of the Father

I was nine years old when I first heard God's voice on my way to school. My family had just begun evening Bible studies in our living room. One night, my stepfather, who knew his time on earth was short, used a cardboard box to explain what heaven might look like. That Sunday, I walked the aisle of our Texas Baptist church and was baptized. The next morning, filled with joy, as I skipped to school, I heard God say, "I will come back to get you. Wait for Me." That was my first encounter with the voice of God.

A few years later, after my stepfather died, we moved to California. I grew up without a father's love, in a home weighed down by alcohol and instability. At nineteen, I married a man who carried his own history of abuse, and that decision led me far from my faith. Twenty years later, divorced and disillusioned, I realized my life was a wreck. In desperation, I returned to church, and again I heard God speak, this time with unmistakable clarity: "Heaven or Hell, choose now."

In that same church, I met the man who would become my husband. He had prayed for a wife, and during a church service he felt God draw his attention to me in the choir. I told him I wasn't dating, but gave him my number anyway. Less than two years later, we were married and raising four children.

Years passed, our children grew, and life seemed settled. Then my body betrayed me. My skin began crawling so badly that I was sent flying out of bed at night, screaming. My friend Daryl saw it happen during a trip meant to give me a break from a previously bedbug-infested home. I thought I was losing my mind, until a doctor diagnosed me with advanced melanoma a week later.

Daryl took me to a healing class where I heard testimonies of miracles. Hope flickered. Rich and I searched for more churches that taught healing, and he eventually found a ministry called Red Seal. There, I sensed God's love in a way that exposed just how wounded my heart had been toward Him. His presence began to make me smile again.

I underwent surgery to remove a malignant spot on my back, hoping it would stop the crawling sensations, but they only worsened. The doctor offered drugs. I refused. "Either God will heal me, or I will die." Then I asked the question no one wants to ask: "God, am I going to die?" His answer came instantly as Scripture in my mind: "I have given you eternal life."

Eight months of torment pushed me closer to God than I had ever been. I went wherever people prayed for healing. I asked for prayer whenever I could. One morning, Rich asked me to take his place in a deliverance class. I felt desperate and begged God, "Do something today. I can't take this anymore."

After the meeting, I asked a woman for prayer. As she prayed, I had to sit just to remain upright. She pressed her hand gently into my side and said, "God wants you to laugh." I began laughing, bewildered, and asked God why I couldn't stop. Then she leaned close to my ear and whispered, "You are not going to die, you will live."

In that moment, I saw God the Father. He was young, full of joy, and laughing as He poked me in the side, repeating those same words. I had never imagined God as fun. The vision dropped me to the floor, laughing and crying until I curled up like a child. The next morning at church, my pastor looked at me and said, "Dianne, you look ten years younger. What happened to you?" After I explained, he quietly walked away. I realized then that God often works outside the boundaries of our theology. He wants us to know Him as He truly is.

My skin improved through prayer, but the crawling would sometimes return. Not wanting to live with this torment, I continued seeking healing. Rich drove me to Bethel Church in Redding. During the evening service, a man sitting nearby said, "You are the one God told me about. You have skin cancer and bitterness." I had told his wife about the cancer, but not my past. When I asked how he knew, he said, "God told me. Ask Him."

I closed my eyes, and memories from my childhood to adulthood flooded me, one after another. When I finally lifted my head, he prayed for me. The crawling sensation changed into bubbles that moved over my head. Shocked, I asked, "What was that?" He replied, "Your healing."

That night, God healed my cancer, tendinitis, and sleep disorder. My faith shifted from a distant one into a new reality. I discovered God as my

Healer and my Father. I began asking Him questions, and He answered. When I asked, "What do You want me to do?" He said, "Write."

This devotional is my response. It was written out of encounters with God, moments of inspiration, and conversations with Him. Afterwards, I looked for Scriptures that matched what He had already spoken to my heart.

My relationship with God had moved into close conversations. One day I asked, "God, what is the most important thing to You? Prayer? Memorizing Scripture? What is it?" Immediately, His answer came: "Knowledge of the Holy One." I wouldn't have thought of that on my own. It was an obscure verse in the Bible that I had to look up.

As I studied, I understood. Knowledge of the Holy One is the history you build with God, the personal moments when you can say, "God did this for me." True knowing comes through encounter. Every time He intervenes, every time He speaks, every time His presence becomes real to you, your knowledge of Him grows.

My prayer is that as you journey through these pages, your own history with God will deepen, and knowing Him will become the greatest adventure of your life.

—Dianne Tylski

January

January 1

The Deep Well

"But whoever drinks of the water that I shall give him will never thirst. But the water that I shall give him will become in him a fountain of water springing up into everlasting life." The woman said to Him, "Sir, give me this water, that I may not thirst, nor come here to draw."
— *John 4:14–15 (NKJV)*

Contemplation:
What is Salvation?

The Response:
In your thirst, draw living water from the deep well of salvation. Within this well flows the living water of My Spirit, My passion for you, My sustaining power, and My incomparable companionship. Let your thirst compel you to ask Me for more. I Am the One who turns dissatisfaction into the sweet knowing of who I Am. I Am the One who speaks with you now.

January 2

My Disciple

> Then He arose and rebuked the wind and the raging of the water. And they ceased, and there was a calm.
> — *Luke 8:24 (NKJV)*

Contemplation:
Lord, will You speak to me?

The Response:
I Am speaking to those I love. Put your trust in Me. Be like Mary and sit at My feet with expectancy. I will place My thoughts within your mind, for I Am willing to speak to your heart. My voice is stronger than your own thoughts. Live with holy expectancy. What do you see and hear that comes from Me? Look to the unseen and listen. Be My disciple and follow Me through the valley of the shadow of death, for I will walk and talk with you there. Do not pass Me by in the storm by thinking I Am not near. Set your mind on Me, and the waves will grow still. Be My disciple.

January 3

A Talk With God

I will both lie down in peace, and sleep; For You alone, O Lord, make me dwell in safety.
—*Psalm 4:8 (NKJV)*

See also: Psalm 38:13-17

Contemplation:
God, this trial is long and wearisome. Am I complaining? Will I die? I need Your comfort, Your joy, power, and more faith. Thank You that I am in Your care. I know my relief will come, but when will it arrive? I am tired.

The Response:
I Am the Faithful and True One. Where is your trust and thankfulness for all I have done? I have given you My promise and My Spirit. Listen, and I will cause you to lie down in peace. I Am your Peace. I have given you eternal life to live in every moment. You need Me. Be willing to confess your unbelief and yield it to Me. Rest completely in My care and choose to trust Me. Guard your mind carefully, for I Am with you and have given you hope. Wait on Me. Believe Me. I Am your help. Yes, yes, My child. You are Mine, irrevocably Mine.

January 4

My Love

Set me as a seal upon your heart, as a seal upon your arm; For love is as strong as death, Jealousy as cruel as the grave; Its flames are flames of fire, A most vehement flame.
— *Song of Songs 8:6 (NKJV)*

Contemplation:
Can I really know Your love?

The Response:
You are My beloved child, sealed in the fullness of My love. Ask for My Spirit to fill every empty place within your heart. When you awaken, let My thoughts settle deep within you, for I think of you far beyond your understanding. In your moments of misery, worship Me and allow My love to comfort you. Live today wrapped in My love, and you will find the joy and strength to continue.

January 5

Hope Is

> Why are you cast down, O my soul? And why are you disquieted within me? Hope in God; For I shall yet praise Him, the help of my countenance and my God.
> —*Psalm 42:5 (NKJV)*

Contemplation:
Lord, will I trust You enough to remain in the safe harbor of hope until I see Your hand working on my behalf?

The Response:
Hope is the refuge I have prepared for you. It is the anchor that keeps your soul steadfast in Me. In hope and trust, Jesus went before you, entering My presence to open the way. So let your soul rest and wait in hope. Trust Me. Let your expectation rise. Be patient and abide in the safe harbor of divine hope. Remain with Me until hope matures into confidence that I Am working faithfully in you. This is the hope that cannot be deferred and will not disappoint, for it is rooted in Me. Watch and see, I Am moving mightily on your behalf.

January 6

Joy Is Lasting

You will show me the path of life;
In Your presence is fullness of joy;
At Your right hand are pleasures forevermore.
—*Psalm 16:11 (NKJV)*

Contemplation:
God, what is real joy?

The Response:
Joy is knowing that eternity is real and lasting. All else is fading away. Joy is the steady flame that remains when every temporary light burns out. It is the song of the soul that remembers where it came from and where it's going. In the awareness of eternity, joy becomes unshakable, for nothing passing can steal what is forever secure in Me.

January 7

Overcoming Love

*He brought me to the banqueting house,
And his banner over me was love.*
— Song of Songs 2:4 (NKJV)

See also: Mark 9:23

Contemplation:
Today, I experienced Your love hovering over me like a cloud. Thinking of it makes me smile.

The Response:
I Am your Father, and you are the child of My choosing. Why do you wrestle against knowing My great love? I have told you that I think of you more often than you think of yourself, so that you may recognize My nearness. What you have felt is the power of My love—an overcoming love that never fails.

Begin today by understanding that you are a vessel needing to be filled with My Spirit. My power is ever present, freely given to those who receive. Accept My gift of healing. When pain comes, declare, "His banner over me is love. I am my Beloved's, and He is mine."

Let your thoughts and actions be transformed as you ponder these truths in your heart. You do not need the comforts of this world, for they cannot cure your misery. Your need is to become an empty vessel that I may fill. I desire your temple. Dwell in My love and goodness, and even the hard things will lose their weight before My glory.

January 8
Matters of the Mind

For I know the thoughts that I think toward you, says the Lord, thoughts of peace and not of evil, to give you a future and a hope.
—*Jeremiah 29:11 (NKJV)*

See also: Romans 8:5-7   Romans 12:2

Contemplation:
God, is there a way out of wrong thinking?

The Response:
Seek My thoughts in every situation.
As you seek My face, I will place My words within you.
My Spirit is given to relieve and refresh your mind.
I Am the One who purifies your thoughts and renews your heart.
From Me comes true wisdom, pure and full of peace.

January 9

Know Me

That Christ may dwell in your hearts through faith; that you, being rooted and grounded in love, may be able to comprehend with all the saints what is *the width and length and depth and height- to know the love of Christ which passes knowledge; that you may be filled with all the fullness of God.*
— *Ephesians 3:17-19 (NKJV)*

See also: Jeremiah 17:7–8   Galatians 5:22

Contemplation:
Lord, here I am in Your presence; do I really know You?

The Response:
You spoke to my heart:
You do know Me, for I have never changed.
I Am your Father.
I Am Healer. I Am here, in this very place.
I Am ever with you.
Be one with Me and delight in My presence.
You are being changed, shaped into a new mind.
Take My hand and the courage I give you.
Believe Me, and you will be blessed.
Step into love, and into a faith that continually increases.

January 10
Come Up Here

Then He who sat on the throne said, "Behold, I make all things new." And He said to me, "Write, for these words are true and faithful."
—*Revelation 21:5 (NKJV)*

See also: Ephesians 1:18-21

Contemplation:
In a dream, I found myself in heaven and felt truly alive for the first time.

The Response:
I Am making all things new.
Believe in My power to restore and remake every part of your life.
Ask Me for more, and you will fulfill My joy.
I have chosen and called you by name to come up higher.
Here, in the heights of My presence, you will see with My eyes, hear with My ears, and feel with My heart.
Here you will discover all that I have prepared for you.
The life of heaven is given to those who seek it.
Know Me in this place, for I will reveal hidden things to you.

January 11

The Secret Place

*For in the time of trouble He shall hide me in His pavilion;
In the secret place of His tabernacle He shall hide me;
He shall set me high upon a rock.
— Psalm 27:5 (NKJV)*

See also: Song of Songs 2:10-13

Contemplation:
I am getting weary, Lord. When will I be healed?

The Response:
Do not dwell on your weakness.
Look instead to My Spirit for comfort.
In your pain and in your hurt, turn your eyes to Me.
I Am the solid Rock—everything you need to rise above the pull of your flesh.
Lift your gaze higher, to My glory.
Come away, My beloved, into the secret place.
Worship Me there, in the heavenly realm, where I share with you the joy of My presence.
In My glory, you will overcome every weakness of the mind.
Let My love overtake you, and in that surrender, you will find My strength.

January 12

Nothing Against

> For God so loved the world that He gave His only begotten Son, that whoever believes in Him should not perish but have everlasting life. For God did not send His Son into the world to condemn the world, but that the world through Him might be saved.
> — *John 3:16–17 (NKJV)*

See also: Isaiah 30:18–21   Romans 10:9–11

Contemplation:
Lord, when will I simply receive the gift of peace and salvation You have already provided for me?

The Response:
I Am the One who has been searching for you.
I long for you to know Me personally.
You have been away too long, but I have made a way for you to return.
I know you by name.
I Am a faithful God who delights in mercy.
I Am love, and I Am just.
Have you forgotten?
You need My peace in your life.
You need to be right with Me.
Are you not tired and weary?
Come back to Me—I have made a way.
Believe Me, for Jesus is the Way, the Truth, and the Life.
He has paid the price for you.
My own Son, whom I love, laid down His life and took it up again.
Through Jesus Christ, you have been given everything you need to be made right with Me.
My peace is a gift to all who place their trust and confidence in what I have done.
Call out to Me, and I will freely pardon you and make your life new.

January 13

Rejoice in Strength

Behold, God is my salvation, I will trust and not be afraid;
'For YAH, the Lord, is my strength and song;
He also has become my salvation.'
— *Isaiah 12:2 (NKJV)*

See also: Exodus 15:2   Psalm 18:2   Psalm 59:17

Contemplation:
Lord, when will I trust You as my strength and delight instead of striving in my own effort?

The Response:
I Am your God, and you are My offspring.
I Am the Rock upon which you stand.
I lift you up and hold your hand.
I Am your strength.
In My steadfast love, remain.
I Am your Fortress and your High Tower.
Look up from the valley and come to the hills.
Look down and see—everything lies beneath your feet.
Trust Me, and do not strive.
From the heights, all is subdued.
Let My strength be your delight.

January 14

Like Esther

> So it was, when the king saw Queen Esther standing in the court, that she found favor in his sight, and the king held out to Esther the golden scepter that was in his hand. Then Esther went near and touched the top of the scepter.
> — *Esther 5:2 (NKJV)*

See also: Esther 5

Contemplation:
God, You look at Your chosen one.
I have obtained Your favor.
Like Esther, I am clothed in majestic apparel.
You have set the royal crown upon my head.

The Response:
I Am your King.
I have called you into My presence and extended My favor to you.
Stand with confidence, for I delight to grant your request and to crown you with My authority.
Do not fear those who oppose you, for My scepter is all you need.
Remain in My presence, and you will witness the reward of My favor unfolding before you.

January 15

Greater Love

"As the Father loved Me, I also have loved you; abide in My love."
— *John 15:9 (NKJV)*

See also: Jeremiah 31:3   Isaiah 54:8-10

Contemplation:
I am delighted in your steadfast love for Me.

The Response:
Let this love keep you rooted in My word, for this is My delight.
I have set My enduring love upon you, and it will never depart.
Let this love of Mine become your longing and your pursuit.
My love shields you from all doubt and despair.
Live in My love, and everything you do will bring honor to Me.
Every victory is born out of great love for Me.

January 16

A Happy Life

> "Come to Me, all you who labor and are heavy laden, and I will give you rest. Take My yoke upon you and learn from Me, for I am gentle and lowly in heart, and you will find rest for your souls. For My yoke is easy and My burden is light."
> — *Matthew 11:28–30 (NKJV)*

See also: Matthew 5:6–12   Romans 14:17

Contemplation:
I had encountered God's love hovering over me. The experience changed how I viewed my circumstances.

The Response:
I Am your satisfaction, and My approval is all you need.
Depend upon Me, and you will have no need for pretense.
Humble yourself among those I bring into your influence, for the poor in spirit reflect My humility.
Learn from Me, for I Am gentle and lowly in heart.
Cry out to Me, and I will comfort you.
Bring to Me all that saddens you, for My Spirit is your constant companion—your help and your friend.
When patience is lacking, ask Me, and I will supply it.
I oppose the self-will of My disciples.
Align your attitude with My Spirit, and I will free you from a critical heart.
I know your desire to stand rightly before Me.
So, walk in joy and peace, and enjoy your new life in Me.

January 17

Walk With Me

As you therefore have received Christ Jesus the Lord, so walk in Him.
— *Colossians 2:6 (NKJV)*

See also: Genesis 6:9   Ephesians 5:15

Contemplation:
Lord, I want to walk closely with You today, aware of Your nearness, instead of being distracted by yesterday or tomorrow.

The Response:
Today, walk with Me and I will give you everything.
Do not doubt Me, but look for the reward found in obedience.
Stay close to Me, for I long for your companionship.
As we move together along the path I have prepared for you, stay aware of My nearness.
Pause often throughout this day and remember what I have spoken to you.
Let today be your only concern.
This continual today is what I meant when I said that Noah walked with Me. Noah found My favor because he walked with Me day by day.
You have asked for My favor, so walk with Me today and your request will be granted.
It is simple, yet within this simplicity lies the truth of our union in eternity.
There is no future or past as we walk together into all that we will become.
The eternal is an ever present now.

January 18

A Returning Heart

*You are my hiding place; You shall preserve me from trouble;
You shall surround me with songs of deliverance.*
— *Psalm 32:7 (NKJV)*

See also: Psalm 32

Contemplation:
God, this is a nightmare from which I cannot wake. Where are You?

The Response:
I have rescued you and revealed many things about Myself.
How can you doubt My love now?
Return your heart to Me, trusting only in My love, and you will flourish.
Your longing for Me is a sweet fragrance that rises before My throne.
Come near, never believing that anything could separate us.
The veil is thin. I Am nearer than your very breath.
Let your love soar upward, for your love is precious to Me.
Even when you do not feel it, I do.
Your love is what I long for—a heart of passion that seeks Me.
This is what heaven is made of.
Yes, by such love you enter even before the appointed time.
Open the heavens with your affection.

January 19

Called to Lead

> But you are a chosen generation, a royal priesthood, a holy nation, His own special people, that you may proclaim the praises of Him who called you out of darkness into His marvelous light; who once were not a people but are now the people of God, who had not obtained mercy but now have obtained mercy.
> — 1 Peter 2:9–10 (NKJV)

Contemplation:
Lord, even the ones who have everything find fault with those who have less.

The Response:
I have not called you to follow others, but to lead them.
Follow Me into truth, and you will walk in joy.
From that joy, you will lead.
I have fashioned you to be like Daniel, for such a time as this.
You will guide those who long to find the freedom and joy My Spirit brings. Keep your eyes on Me, and become all that I have designed you to be—a child of Mine, free to serve Me in joy.

January 20

Declare Victory

> But thanks be to God, who gives us the victory through our Lord Jesus Christ.
> — *1 Corinthians 15:57 (NKJV)*

See also: 1 Samuel 17:45–50   Psalm 98:1   2 Timothy 4:8

Contemplation:
Lord, will I stand and declare the victory You have already won for me in the midst of this battle?

The Response:
I have called you into this battle for the sake of strength.
True strength is not formed in ease, but in resistance.
I Am your God, and the battle belongs to Me.
I have already won it for you, so take up the sword of truth and stand firm.
Declare your victory—shout it aloud!
You will see your enemy fall.
Be the victor I have called you to be, and you will rejoice in Me.
Remember, there is laid up for you the victor's crown.

January 21

Love's Reality

The Lord your God in your midst,
The Mighty One, will save;
He will rejoice over you with gladness,
He will quiet you with His love,
He will rejoice over you with singing.
— *Zephaniah 3:17 (NKJV)*

See also: Psalm 45:1   Song of Songs 2:10

Contemplation:
I was not healed, yet I was suddenly happy in spite of my skin crawling, because I had discovered a new reality.

The Response:
My tongue is the pen of a ready writer.
I must declare this—my love for You burns like fire!
I have loved You with my mind, but now I feel Your love surrounding my heart.
The experience of Your love has changed me forever.
Now I am in love with the Lover of my soul.
My soul sings back to You the very song You sing over me.
I am loved by a perfect Lover who has overwhelmed me with a great and endless love—a love I never knew before.
Our love is now a living reality.
Come, dear Savior, let us slip away again to be alone—just You and I.
Hide me in the cleft of the Rock, where Your arms surround me and Your love becomes tangible, a thick cloud I am allowed to enter.
I am in love with the Lover of my soul!
You are my delight, and my love is Your joy.
We have become one—a great love made real.

January 22

Song of Heaven

They sing the song of Moses, the servant of God, and the song
of the Lamb, saying:
'Great and marvelous are Your works,
Lord God Almighty!
Just and true are Your ways,
O King of the saints!
Who shall not fear You, O Lord, and glorify Your name?
For You alone are holy.
For all nations shall come and worship before You,
For Your judgments have been manifested.'
— *Revelation 15:3–4 (NKJV)*

See also: Revelation 15:2–4

Contemplation:
I will sing the song of love, sung to the One who is enthroned. It is the song of angels above.

The Response:
There is a song given to the sons of Adam—a song of Love come to earth, of Jesus ransoming the sons of men.
Release your joy and enter in, for heaven sings back your anthem.
Let praise echo the sound of heaven!
Jesus—this is the love song: the One who is, who was, and who is to come.
Sing the love of Jesus, for it is the song of heaven given to the sons of men.

January 23

A New Pathway

Then Jesus spoke to them again, saying, 'I am the light of the world. He who follows Me shall not walk in darkness, but have the light of life.'
— *John 8:12 (NKJV)*

See also: Psalm 89:15   Proverbs 12:28

Contemplation:
Lord, I want to walk in the light of Your presence today, trusting the way that You have laid out for me.

The Response:
There is a pathway perfectly prepared for you alone.
Follow it with anticipation, holding My Word in your hand, for everything along this way has been arranged for your good.
Go with Me in joy upon this beautiful path—the one I have prepared for the one I love.
Let nothing hinder you.
Walk without fear or doubt, for now is the time to step into greater light and life.
I Am leading you into glory for My name's sake.
Look ahead and see the light of My countenance shining upon the road before you.
Take time to enjoy your walk with Me, for every step with Me is holy.

January 24

Miracles

God also bearing witness both with signs and wonders, with various miracles, and gifts of the Holy Spirit, according to His own will.
— *Hebrews 2:4 (NKJV)*

See also: Acts 5:12   1 Corinthians 12:10–11   1 Corinthians 12:28

Contemplation:
Many say that we do not need miracles because we have the Bible. What do You say?

The Response:
You must know Me as I Am—the God of Wonders.
In the miraculous, I reveal Myself.
Read the miracles recorded in My Word, for everything I do and have done is miraculous.
You are a miracle, created by My own design.
I became one with humanity through a miraculous birth.
I healed all who came to Me, that you might know Me as the God of miracles—the One who died and rose again.
Ask Me for greater faith.
Ask, and keep on asking, for miracles.
Faith embraces the impossible, and miracles reveal who I Am.

January 25

Heart of Fire

Let us draw near with a true heart in full assurance of faith, having our hearts sprinkled from an evil conscience and our bodies washed with pure water.
— *Hebrews 10:22 (NKJV)*

See also: Psalm 73:1   Matthew 5:8

Contemplation:
Lord, My desire is this freedom that comes from a pure heart.

The Response:
Out of a purified heart comes the revelation of who I Am and the fullness of My goodness.
Your heart shapes what you do, what you think, how you feel, and how you see others.
It even determines how you see Me.
I treasure the purity of heart.
From a pure heart, I form My kindness, love, and patience within you.
All that I Am flows through a heart made clean, allowing you to walk in true freedom.
Begin here: when dealing with others, come to Me without fear—bring your heart before Me.
Ask Me for a pure heart, and I will fulfill your request.
I will never condemn or rebuke you for asking.
Instead, I will ignite a holy fire within you, burning away every impure motive and thought.
Check your heartbeat.
I desire to give your heart a rhythm that beats with Mine.

January 26

Heart Surrender

> Many waters cannot quench love,
> Nor can floods drown it.
> If a man would give for love
> All the wealth of his house,
> It would be utterly despised.
> — *Song of Songs 8:7 (NKJV)*

See also: Luke 3:16

Contemplation:
God, I want to really know You.

The Response:
Be willing to offer Me what I show you, and lay it upon the altar.
Surrender is the fuel that keeps My fire burning upon your heart—a fire that many waters cannot quench.
You will discover that the storms of life do not shake a surrendered heart.
Lay everything upon the altar, and I will purify your heart.
From this daily surrender and awareness of Me, a strong and steadfast love will rise within you.

January 27

A New Surety

Then He arose and rebuked the wind, and said to the sea, 'Peace, be still!' And the wind ceased and there was a great calm.
— *Mark 4:39 (NKJV)*

See also: Psalm 107:29–30   Matthew 14:29

Contemplation:
God, when will this trial end?

The Response:
If you fix your eyes on the storms, you will be overcome and sink into distress.
But I Am with you, and I have given you all that I Am.
I Am your anchor and your shelter, and I will bring you safely into harbor.
Where I Am, there is always the hope of peace.
Now rise, and command the wind and the waves to be still in My name.
Walk in a faith that declares, "No harm will come to those who are with Me."
I have rescued you from death, and I will rescue you again.
Look to Me, and you will walk upon the waters in the midst of the storm.
I Am calling you to a new place of surety in Me—a place that does not fear, but believes.
You cannot learn to trust Me while standing upon the shore of life.

January 28

In Love

> Let him kiss me with the kisses of his mouth—
> For your love is better than wine.
> —*Song of Songs 1:2 (NKJV)*

See also: Romans 8:39   Jude 1:21

Contemplation:
In Your approval, I find satisfaction for my soul.
Your sweet love fills the deepest places of who I am.
Love is the great discovery that never leaves.
Love sees me and believes.
In Your kindness and patience, I find bliss.
In love, my soul is lifted and satisfied.
It's You I kiss.
I am not denied a view that ends—High above the earth, where love transcends.

The Response:
I have set My love upon you, and nothing can separate you from it.
Rest in the sweetness of My approval, for My love lifts you higher than the pull of this world.
Remain in Me, and you will know the joy of a love that never ends.

January 29

Do All in My Name

*Commit your works to the Lord,
And your thoughts will be established.*
— *Proverbs 16:3 (NKJV)*

See also: John 14:12   Ephesians 2:10

Contemplation:
I need to see what You are doing.

The Response:
I Am always at work in your life.
What you consider small are, to Me, great works.
This is the law of My kingdom—I see differently than you do.
Take joy in all that I do, and work each day in the strength I provide.

January 30

Within the Veil

> This hope we have as an anchor of the soul, both sure and steadfast, and which enters the Presence behind the veil.
> — *Hebrews 6:19 (NKJV)*

See also: Hebrews 9:3   Hebrews 10:20

Contemplation:
I will sing to You from my soul.
I will worship until Your presence draws near.
Lord, I will adore You within the veil.
Now, here at Your feet, Your presence surrounds me.
As Your glory descends, all is well.
Lord, my heart cries out within the veil.
Deep cries to deep in this holy place.
Look—angels are dancing all around, while I am in Your presence, where You are glorious. Just You and I, standing on holy ground.
Sing, my soul, until all fades into wonder.
I will sing from my spirit, "All is well."
Lord, I worship You here, within the veil.

The Response:
I Am your anchor—steady and unshakable—drawing you behind the veil into My presence.
Here you will find glory, peace, and the joy of communion with Me.
Remain near, and you will know that all is truly well.

January 31

Peace

*These things I have spoken to you, that in Me you may have peace.
In the world you will have tribulation; but be of good cheer, I
have overcome the world.*
— *John 16:33 (NKJV)*

See also: Isaiah 9:6   Romans 15:13

Contemplation:
God, how am I going to survive this trial? My suffering is too difficult and long.

The Response:
I Am the Prince of Peace.
All that you need to endure and overcome in this world is found in My Name.
I came to bring peace, and My peace I have left with you—a parting gift that remains forever.
Renew your friendship with Me by abiding in My peace.
Agree that I Am able to keep you safe and secure from all harm.
Then your storm will cease to rise, and the waves will grow calm.
Perfect peace is My presence within you.
Seek Peace, and you will find Me.

February 1

The Promise

Therefore we do not lose heart. Even though our outward man is perishing, yet the inward man is being renewed day by day. For our light affliction, which is but for a moment, is working for us a far more exceeding and eternal weight of glory.
— *2 Corinthians 4:16–17 (NKJV)*

See also: 2 Peter 1:3   Revelation 22:12

I have promised you that your burden here is producing an everlasting reward. All that is unseen is what is lasting, and eternal; everything else is fading away. Let Me renew your mind each day, and you will have the strength to carry on. Trust Me in these days of distress. Look with Me to all that is eternal and let My love sustain you. I Am preparing you for more than you know. This transformation will surprise you. Take courage and let hope arise. You really do possess all things that are Life.

February 2

Expect Great Things

Delight yourself also in the LORD,
And He shall give you the desires of your heart.
Commit your way to the LORD,
Trust also in Him,
And He shall bring *it* to pass.
— *Psalm 37:4-5 (NKJV)*

See also: Psalm 62:5   Isaiah 40:31   Philippians 1:6

A child looks to the one who can care for them with confident expectation. Wait on Me in hope, where you will find strength in expectancy. I do far above what you want of Me. Have I ever failed you? You must remain in faith. At the beginning of the day, wait to hear from Me, and you will learn to live in daily expectancy. As your experience of Me increases, you will know Me as I Am. The God of miracles. It is My joy to give you great things. I love you, My child.

February 3

My Prophet

> Therefore Eli said to Samuel, 'Go, lie down; and it shall be, if He calls you, that you must say, "Speak, Lord, for Your servant hears."' So Samuel went and lay down in his place. Now the Lord came and stood and called as at other times, 'Samuel! Samuel!' And Samuel answered, 'Speak, for Your servant hears.'
> — *1 Samuel 3:9–10 (NKJV)*

See also: 1 Corinthians 1:26–29

I Am the One who has chosen you and caused you to come near to Me. Come nearer still, in reverence, waiting to hear My voice. Seek My presence, and you will speak for Me as Samuel did. I desire to have faithful servants in My house. Wait on Me.
Just say, "Here I am, Lord."
And I will respond, "Speak, for I Am listening."
Learn the art of remaining in My presence until I come. Listen and obey Me. Speak My words of life and encourage all My household to do the same. Carefully train your mind and heart and confess your need of Me, then I will give you a word to encourage another. Guard your heart against any judgments of your own. These are important days to Me. Be a chosen vessel and sanctify your heart to Me again, for I have chosen you to be a voice in these last days.

February 4

Real Love

And now abide faith, hope, love, these three; but the greatest of these is love.
— *1 Corinthians 13:13 (NKJV)*

Contemplation:
When things go wrong, God, where are You?

The Response:
I Am Love. I will reveal Myself to you as you seek to understand Me. Our relationship is more important than your thoughts on life's difficulties. Our love needs to be tested and tried in this life. My love must overcome every irritant. Choose Love in every situation. Know that I Am for you, as you believe that My love conquers all. Someday, what seems important will vanish, and you will know that Love was the truth you were seeking. Choose to become a reflection of Me. Let My love sustain you.

February 5

Identity

Blessed be the God and Father of our Lord Jesus Christ, who has blessed us with every spiritual blessing in the heavenly places in Christ, just as He chose us in Him before the foundation of the world, that we should be holy and without blame before Him in love, having predestined us to adoption as sons by Jesus Christ to Himself, according to the good pleasure of His will, to the praise of the glory of His grace, by which He made us accepted in the Beloved. In Him we have redemption through His blood, the forgiveness of sins, according to the riches of His grace which He made to abound toward us in all wisdom and prudence, having made known to us the mystery of His will, according to His good pleasure which He purposed in Himself.
— *Ephesians 1:3-9 (NKJV)*

I Myself picked you out of the whole world to be My own, so that you could stand blameless before Me in love. This is My kind intent, to give you the destiny that I have planned out for you as My dear child in Christ. So praise Me for all the favor I have bestowed on you so freely in My Beloved Son!
In My Son's blood, you have salvation and forgiveness for all your shortcomings and offenses. I Am rich in mercy, and I Am generous with My favor. I lavish every grace upon you and give you My wisdom so that you can have insight into your own identity.

February 6

Study To Look Away

And Elisha prayed, and said, "Lord, I pray, open his eyes that he may see." Then the Lord opened the eyes of the young man, and he saw. And behold, the mountain was full of horses and chariots of fire all around Elisha.
—*2 Kings 6:17 (NKJV)*

See also: 2 Corinthians 3:17-18   2 Corinthians 4:2-18

Turn your gaze—and don't look back.
In Hebrew, the root shaʿah means to gaze, to regard, to turn one's sight. It even carries the sense of looking away from distractions.
You must lift your eyes from the temporary and fix them on the eternal, so you see the larger reality. Look through the veil to the unseen realm where I dwell. That is where My life flows.
Just as Elisha glimpsed into the spiritual dimension, let your heart believe. Pray for sight. Ask Me to pierce the darkness with light. Imagine with Me. Turn your attention away from all that is lesser, to behold My face.
Let me show you the eternal treasures of heaven. Lay down each distraction. Come away with Me, my beloved. I will become your reality. Nothing is impossible in this place. Come and see.

February 7

Kingdom Laws

**A man's heart plans his way,
But the Lord directs his steps.**
—Proverbs 16:9 (NKJV)

See also: Ephesians 2:10

I Am at work in your life.
The things you deem small are the greater works that I Am doing.
This is the law of My kingdom. I see things differently.
Take joy in doing all, great or small.
Work in My strength every day.
I have chosen you to be a blessing.
Greater things are coming for you to do.

February 8

The Glory Of Purity

But 'he who glories, let him glory in the Lord.'
— *2 Corinthians 10:17 (NKJV)*

See also: Jeremiah 9:24

If you must glory, then glory in this—that you understand Me.
Glory in knowing Me, both personally and practically.
Glory in hearing My voice.
Glory in abiding in My presence.
Glory in discerning and knowing My character.
Be Mine in a covenant of inward purity.

February 9

A Love That Constrains

Lord, You have heard the desire of the humble;
You will prepare their heart;
You will cause Your ear to hear.
— *Psalm 10:17 (NKJV)*

See also: Psalm 20:4   Psalm 91:14   Colossians 1:10

Contemplation:
I desire to know Jesus more deeply and fully.

The Response:
This desire within you is the one I Myself have placed in your heart.
Oh, how dear you are to Me!
I have set My love upon you simply because I chose to do so.
When you were born, I looked upon you with love, and My love has never wavered.
It is steadfast and sure.
Rejoice and trust in this love that is filled with mercy and truth.
Apart from trusting My love, you cannot fully understand it, for it is too great to be comprehended—only experienced.
My love must be trusted through your encounters with Me.
Intimacy is required.
So respond to My love, and let that love constrain your heart and open your eyes to see Us as one.

February 10

Mercy

**Praise the Lord!
Oh, give thanks to the Lord, for He is good!
For His mercy endures forever.**
— *Psalm 106:1 (NKJV)*

See also: Luke 18:13   James 2:13

Humble yourself and draw near to Me, bowing low in heart and mind. I will lift you up in My mercy and love. My kindness reaches deeper than your failings, and My mercy will free you from every bondage.

In My mercy and love, you are made whole and healed as you admit your failings and helplessness. Come into My presence, beating upon your breast, saying, "Oh Lord, have mercy on me, a sinner." Bow your knee, lower your head, even weep if you must.

Come to Me in this posture, and I will justify you, making you right before Me in love. You will go your way lifted up, with a joyful heart. In My forgiveness, you have found mercy, and in My mercy, you are loved.

Be watchful, for pride continually rises to war against My Spirit. Let humility be your protection and mercy your song.

February 11

All Things New

Therefore we were buried with Him through baptism into death, that just as Christ was raised from the dead by the glory of the Father, even so we also should walk in newness of life.
— *Romans 6:4 (NKJV)*

See also: 2 Corinthians 5:17   Revelation 21:5-7

Why do you keep looking for Me among the deadness of your past? I intend to give you a newness of mind and heart. I Am saying to you, *"See, I make all things new!"*

A fresh wind of My Spirit is blowing. Let it carry away the old thoughts that have kept you from My presence. I will keep you close by My side, for I Am your protection and strength.

No longer give place to lies or doubts—laugh at the enemy, for his day is done. This is a new day! Take hold of it in the power of My Name and by My authority. You possess the Sword of My Spirit; wield it boldly and make a path for newness of life.

When the new comes, rejoice and be delighted, for I see you free and laughing with Me.

February 12

The Kingdom

The field is the world, the good seeds are the sons of the kingdom, but the tares are the sons of the wicked one. *The enemy who sowed them is the devil, the harvest is the end of the age, and the reapers are the angels.*
— *Matthew 13:38-39 (NKJV)*

See also: Matthew 13:3-9   Mark 4:14-20

My kingdom is the field I have purchased and sown with seed. Do not think this field excludes you, for it is made up of all who hear My word and believe. You have chosen to believe Me, and more will be given to you. The evil one will no longer snatch away what I have spoken through unbelief. Pursue Me and let your roots grow deep, so that when trouble or persecution comes, it will not steal your trust or your joy.

You are the good seed that blesses the world, for My eternal kingdom is at hand. Be found tending My field, for I Am looking for a harvest! I have called for the banqueting table to be set—go and invite all to come in.

Do not be limited by the doctrines of men that close the gates of heaven. It is My good pleasure to give you the keys of the kingdom. Open wide what I have freely given, and watch My kingdom grow.

February 13

The Days Of Noah

But as the days of Noah were, so also will the coming of the Son of Man be. For as in the days before the flood, they were eating and drinking, marrying and giving in marriage, until the day that Noah entered the ark.
— *Matthew 24:37-38 (NKJV)*

See also: Luke 17:26   1 Peter 3:20-22   Jude 1:21

I Am the Prince of Peace.
In these days of evil, let your mind rest in peace, knowing that I Am accomplishing all things.
Your part is to cooperate with Me by refusing to join in dissension.
Stay clear of the turmoil by keeping your mind fixed on Me.
Keep your mouth from speaking guile, and you will be free from the ills that make many weary of life.
Seek the lighter and higher life by awakening your spirit to Mine.
These are the days of Noah, and you must rise above the storm.
Stay with Me on the ark of My love, surrounded by My presence.
Here, you will float gently above the waves.
Your calmness will be seen.
Your joy and your strength will be renewed.

Ask Me for the love you need in these days, for I desire that you be known by My love and compassion.
I long to give you a heart that sees others as I see them.

February 14

Wonderful

Then Manoah said to the Angel of the Lord, "What is Your name, that when Your words come to pass we may honor You?"
And the Angel of the Lord said to him, "Why do you ask My name, seeing it is wonderful?"
— *Judges 13:17-18 (NKJV)*

See also: Isaiah 9:6   Isaiah 25:1

I Am the God of wonders! In the wilderness, I revealed Myself to My people through miracles and by the marvelous ways I provided for them. I led them by day with a cloud of glory and by night with a pillar of fire for their protection. I Am still the same.
Be like Joshua of old, who lingered after Moses in the tent of meeting, unwilling to leave My presence. In the sanctuary, I will give you the same faith, courage, and blessing, making you able to lead others who walk in fear or doubt.
As you worship Me, I will reveal Myself to you in greater ways. You will know Me as Wonderful, and you will declare aloud, "Your Name is Wonderful!"

February 15

Newness

That which is born of the flesh is flesh, and that which is born of the Spirit is spirit. Do not marvel that I said to you, 'You must be born again.'
— *John 3:6-7 (NKJV)*

See also: 2 Corinthians 5:17   Revelation 3:11

Believe Me when I say that you are a vessel of Mine—chosen and set apart to accomplish the works appointed to you by the Father's decree. Let new things come to you as I reveal them by My Spirit. Everything I do in your life is for My glory and for your rejoicing.

You have asked for a crown to cast before Me, and I Am preparing you by placing a crown upon your head. I see you as My bride, radiant in beauty, adorned for our wedding day.

Arise from the ashes of the lies you once believed, and let the wind of My Spirit blow them away. Behold, I Am forever bringing you into the newness of life. Walk in that newness, and let your joy reflect the glory of the One who renews all things.

February 16

Do You Have Any Bread?

"When I broke the five loaves for the five thousand, how many baskets full of fragments did you take up?"
They said to Him, "Twelve."
"Also, when I broke the seven for the four thousand, how many large baskets full of fragments did you take up?"
And they said, "Seven."
So He said to them, "How is it you do not understand?"
— *Mark 8:19-21 (NKJV)*

My disciples gathered twelve small baskets of leftovers after I fed the five thousand—one basket for each of them, a reminder of My faithfulness.
But when I fed the four thousand, there were seven large provision baskets collected.
There were seven small loaves and seven abundant baskets—symbols of heaven's overflowing supply.
The large baskets contained far more than the small hand baskets.
So share in My kingdom from what remains of your personal dining with Me.
Give to others from the overflow of your communion with Me.
You will also give from the large baskets—the abundance of My blessings in your life.
When I give you more, give more.
This is the law of heaven, and the number is seven.
I sustain you, and I bless you abundantly.
You will be blessed when I find you supplying food to My household.
Tell Me, how many baskets are in your hand?

February 17

Son of Love

> Then David comforted Bathsheba his wife, and went in to her and lay with her. So she bore a son, and he called his name Solomon. Now the Lord loved him, and He sent word by the hand of Nathan the prophet: So he called his name Jedidiah, because of the Lord.
> — *2 Samuel 12:24-25 (NKJV)*

Every time I see your heart, I smile. You are a son of My favor, for in you I find great kindness. The enemy has tried many times to take this heart from you with many wounds, and has pierced your heart with many trials and adversities.

I Am coming to your aid now. Reach out your hand, and I will mend and restore all. Only believe Me when I say I Am Good and you are dearly loved. Be to Me a son, for I Am to you a Father. Talk to Me often and bring to Me your circumstances. I Am longing to give you more understanding.

February 18

God Is Good

Ask, and it will be given to you; seek, and you will find; knock, and it will be opened to you. For everyone who asks receives, and he who seeks finds, and to him who knocks it will be opened. Or what man is there among you who, if his son asks for bread, will give him a stone? Or if he asks for a fish, will he give him a serpent? If you then, being evil, know how to give good gifts to your children, how much more will your Father who is in heaven give good things to those who ask Him!
— *Matthew 7:7-11 (NKJV)*

See also: John 14:13-14

Contemplation:
How good are You, God?

The Response:
I Am the source of every good thing.
In My goodness, you have been redeemed.
Ask of Me—believing—for all that you need, and even more besides.
Know Me as I Am: your good Father.
Keep on asking, keep on seeking, keep on knocking.
Be a child of faith.
And know this in every way—I Am good!

February 19

A Pure Heart

With the pure You will show Yourself pure;
And with the devious You will show Yourself shrewd.
— *2 Samuel 22:27 (NKJV)*

See also: Psalm 51:7   Titus 1:15   James 3:17

My heart is pure love, woven with all that is just and right.
Wisdom from above flows out of a pure heart.
I have promised you many things, but My greatest desire is this—to place My own heart within you, to purify your life through the reality of My Word and My Presence.
Come to Me with your heart, that I may purify it.
My love is the consuming fire you have longed for.
In worship, keep your heart open, close enough to hear My heartbeat.
Then you will know My love, for it will flow from the very heart of Mine within you.

February 20

Blessings

**Keep me as the apple of Your eye;
Hide me under the shadow of Your wings.**
— Psalm 17:8 (NKJV)

See also: Numbers 22:12-20   Matthew 5:44

You are Mine, and you have chosen to camp around My altar, drawing near to Me. Wherever you see those who, like Balaam, would prophesy for hire, know that jealousy, fear, and envy are at work. I Am teaching you to discern what is good, for evil abounds in many disguises.

Bless others—even your enemies. Never let anything be found on your lips but a blessing, and I will bless you sevenfold. Be My prophet by speaking only what I instruct you to say.

You dwell under the shadow of My wing, together with others who gather around My glory. Here you will learn to love deeply and to forgive every offense. In this place of mercy, you will bless both yourself and others, as I continually add to your welfare and peace.

February 21

Refining Love

And the Angel of the Lord appeared to him in a flame of fire from the midst of a bush. So he looked, and behold, the bush was burning with fire, but the bush was not consumed.
— *Exodus 3:2 (NKJV)*

See also: Proverbs 17:3   Hebrews 12:29   2 Timothy 1:6

I Am the Refiner's Fire.
I Am still the same—out of the fire I spoke to Moses, and out of the fire of My Word I have spoken to you, My disciple.
Fan into flame the passion I have placed within you.
Remember the words I have spoken to your heart and mind.
You are Mine, and My desire is to cast fire upon the earth through your passion for Me.
It is written: My angels are messengers and flames of fire.
I have sent them to aid you, to bring the fire of My presence upon the earth.
I look for you to carry that flame—the very fire kindled by My words spoken to you.
So I say again, fan the flame I have lit within you through all that I have revealed.
Do not let any hindrance stifle this message.
Press on, and all will become clear as you trust Me.
Faith must pass through the fire of My refining love.
Do not hinder Me, for I Am doing a great work.

February 22

As My Esther

For if you remain completely silent at this time, relief and deliverance will arise for the Jews from another place, but you and your father's house will perish. Yet who knows whether you have come to the kingdom for such a time as this.
– Esther 4:14 (NKJV)

See also: Esther 8:4-13

As Esther, I have chosen you, clothed you in royal apparel, and set a crown upon your head to rule with Me.
You have obtained My favor.
Do not fear when the authority I have given you is challenged, for this world continually seeks to cast off My laws.
Now is the time to pray.
I hold out My scepter to you, granting your request—your petition to stay the enemy and to wait for My perfect timing.
I have sealed your destiny.
You will reign with Me, My Esther, for the time of deliverance is now.

February 23

Salt Poured Out

For everyone will be seasoned with fire, and every sacrifice will be seasoned with salt. Salt is good, but if the salt loses its flavor, how will you season it? Have salt in yourselves, and peace with one another.
—Mark 9:49–50 (NKJV)

See also: Romans 12:1

The salt poured upon you is a symbol of My lasting protection.
It is meant to preserve your life and our covenant relationship.
In consecration and in purification, you are set apart for Me.
My desire is to see fire in your eyes and purity in your life.
I Am your portion forever—your inheritance among holy things.
I have impressed upon your heart a deep sense of your indebtedness to Me.
You owe Me everything.
So give to Me all that you are and all that you hope to become.
I will heal your wounds and bind up the brokenness within you.

February 24

Two Trees

> Then the Lord God said, "Behold, the man has become like one of Us, to know good and evil. And now, lest he put out his hand and take also of the tree of life, and eat, and live forever"— therefore the Lord God sent him out of the garden of Eden to till the ground from which he was taken. So He drove out the man; and He placed cherubim at the east of the garden of Eden, and a flaming sword which turned every way, to guard the way to the tree of life.
> — *Genesis 3:22-24 (NKJV)*

See also: Proverbs 11:30   Matthew 12:33   Revelation 2:7

Seek the Tree of Wisdom, for from it you will partake of all that I Am. No one may eat of this tree except those who come boldly, seeking Me with a pure heart. All My ways are designed to draw you deeper into wisdom and truth. Lay hold of Me and remain faithful to My words. Seek Me above mere knowledge, for knowledge alone cannot give life. Those who rely on their own understanding will go hungry, but those who learn of Me will eat and be satisfied.

The Tree of Life is watered from My sanctuary, bearing life-giving fruit for your nourishment and healing. I guard this place with flaming swords of truth, protecting you from the accusations of the enemy.

You are known by the fruit your life produces—let it reveal that you have eaten from My tree.

February 25

Fun In The Son

"But let him who glories glory in this,
That he understands and knows Me,
That I *am* the LORD, exercising lovingkindness, judgment, and righteousness in the earth.
For in these I delight," says the LORD.
— *Jeremiah 9:24 (NKJV)*

Contemplation:
My question: "God, are You fun?"

The Response:
My answer to you is yes—and amen!
I Am the Creator of joy. I delight in you, and I rejoice over you with gladness. I long for you to enjoy Me as much as I enjoy you.
Take time to remember the moments when you've felt My joy. I have many surprises reserved for you, treasures hidden in the ordinary. Look to Me as a child—with outstretched arms and a heart full of wonder. Anticipate the surprises waiting in each new day, for this is the abundant life I have promised you.
You are dear to Me, and I created you to live in oneness with Me.
Remember this: Have fun today. When you smile, think of Me—because I'm smiling too.

February 26

Set Free

But now having been set free from sin, and having become servants of God, you have your fruit to holiness, and the end, everlasting life.
– Romans 6:22 (NKJV)

See also: 2 Corinthians 3:17   Galatians 5:1

You are free in My Spirit to become and to do all that I created you for.
I will make your burden light and give you rest.
So rest now, and know that I lead you in paths that are not hard.
I go before you, for I Am the Way.
All I ask is that you surrender everything to Me.
I want you to live free—truly free.
Walk in the freedom of My Spirit.
Listen to Me when I say: you have made the easy hard through your own thinking.
My way is easy.
I will take your hand and lift you up into newness of life—free from self-criticism and fear.
This is the day of freedom.
Say with Me now: "The chains are broken; My burdens lifted!"

February 27

Watching You

For the eyes of the Lord run to and fro throughout the whole earth, to show Himself strong on behalf of those whose heart is loyal to Him. In this you have done foolishly; therefore from now on you shall have wars.
— *2 Chronicles 16:9 (NKJV)*

See also: Psalm 11:4   Psalm 34:15

My eye is on you. Do not imagine that I do not see you.
You are ever before Me in love. Instead of watching others or imagining that others are watching you, see Me watching you! Only as you see Me watching you will you be free from your bondage of the fear of man. Your critical thinking will be corrected when you think of My eyes beholding only you!
Look into My eyes and see Me, in love, watching you.
One look of yours is what I long for.
I watch and wait for you to return My glances.
Return My love and look!

February 28

The Ripple Effect

**So shall My word be that goes forth from My mouth;
It shall not return to Me void,
But it shall accomplish what I please,
And it shall prosper** *in the thing* **for which I sent it.**
— *Isaiah 55:11 (NKJV)*

See also: Isaiah 45:23   Romans 4:21

Look at the water of your life as I cast the pebble of My Word into it. Each word I speak creates ripples that move outward with power, touching every part of your circumstances.

My Word never stops at the point of impact—it flows outward, reaching many beyond you, influencing hearts and lives again and again. It performs all that I have purposed to do.

So, cast My Word boldly into your life. Speak it, believe it, and watch what I will accomplish in and through you. My Word never returns void but moves like ripples upon the water—ever expanding, ever working, ever fulfilling My will.

Take notice and ponder the beauty of My work within you, for every ripple carries the power of My promise.

February 29

Walk In White

After these things the word of the Lord came to Abram in a vision, saying, "Do not be afraid, Abram. I am your shield, your exceedingly great reward."
— *Genesis 15:1 (NKJV)*

See also: Colossians 1:10   Revelation 3:18-21

You are called by My Name, and I have made you worthy. Separate yourself from all that would contaminate your heart and mind. I Am your exceeding great reward, and I delight when you find joy in all that is of Me.

I give you rest as you purpose in your heart to know Me—not through sacrifice, but through love. Let Me fill your thoughts, and you will remain kept in My love.

See yourself standing before Me, clothed in white—pure, accepted, and radiant in My presence. Stay there, in the confidence of My acceptance, for this is where peace and holiness dwell together.

March 1

Take the Stage

Therefore do not cast away your confidence, which has great reward. For you have need of endurance, so that after you have done the will of God, you may receive the promise.
— *Hebrews 10:35–36 (NKJV)*

I see you as a rare violin, hauntingly beautiful, carved from wood once beaten and scarred yet shaped by the Master Craftsman. From what was broken, He draws forth a melody unlike any other, a sound both tender and powerful.
This is the Master's workmanship—His divine skill transforming the damaged, the flawed, and the rescued into a one-of-a-kind instrument with a voice uniquely her own.
In God's hands, her life becomes a rare instrument of grace, releasing a sound the world is waiting to hear.
God is calling you—take the stage!

March 2

You Belong to Me

Mercy and truth have met together;
Righteousness and peace have kissed.
— *Psalm 85:10 (NKJV)*

See also: Proverbs 3:3   Matthew 16:18   John 21:22   Galatians 6:4-7

You belong to Me first, not to each other. Why do you look to another as if they stand above Me? I say to you, "What does that matter to you? Follow Me."
I do not see My Body as divided. You err when you doubt that the gates of hell will not prevail against My Church. I Am still in charge of every member of My Body. Your opinion is not required—your obedience is.
Examine your heart for mercy, and there you will find truth.

March 3

Call of My Heart

But the Lord said to Samuel, "Do not look at his appearance or at his physical stature, because I have refused him. For the Lord does not see as man sees; for man looks at the outward appearance, but the Lord looks at the heart."
— *1 Samuel 16:7 (NKJV)*

See also: 1 Chronicles 28:9   Psalm 24:3-4   Proverbs 4:23   Matthew 5:8

I Am always concerned about the state of your heart. I have provided peace for your mind, but your heart must belong fully to Me. I have told you that I search your mind, but I test your heart, for out of your heart flow the issues of life.
A pure heart releases purity in every word you speak. When your heart is right, your mind will follow. I have given you both a new heart and a new mind—rejoice that you are born anew into this living way.
All those with a pure heart see Me; believe Me. Do not let your heart be troubled or condemned, for with your heart you have laid hold of salvation. Listen to the call of My heart to yours, and answer it often.

March 4

Knowledge of the One

> Then you will understand the fear of the Lord,
> And find the knowledge of God.
> — *Proverbs 2:5 (NKJV)*

See also: Proverbs 9:10   Hosea 6:3-6

Contemplation:
What is the most important thing to You, God?

The Response:
I Am the Holy One who gives beauty to your life. Knowledge of Me goes beyond the mind and the words of men. Your soul longs for the revelation of who I Am to you. Every encounter with Me draws you into a deeper reality of who I Am.

In times of desperation, your knowledge of Me increases. Out of impossible situations, you have come to see that it was My hand upon your life that rescued you. Look and see Me in the memories of your soul.

There you will discover what I value most—*knowledge of the Holy One.*

March 5

In the Boat

For He commands and raises the stormy wind,
Which lifts up the waves of the sea.
They mount up to the heavens,
They go down again to the depths;
Their soul melts because of trouble.
They reel to and fro, and stagger like a drunken man,
And are at their wits' end.
Then they cry out to the Lord in their trouble,
And He brings them out of their distresses.
He calms the storm,
So that its waves are still.
Then they are glad because they are quiet;
So He guides them to their desired haven.
— *Psalm 107:25-30 (NKJV)*

See also: Mark 4:36-40

Are we not in this boat together, you and I? You do not need to wake Me.
I Am able to keep you, for this is who I Am.
Be still, and know that I Am your safety. Every situation is under My command.
I will bring you out of your distress with a word—a rebuke to your storm: *"Hush now. Peace, be still!"*
Then you will be glad, and your heart will rest in Me.

March 6

Great Mercy

*Let not mercy and truth forsake you;
Bind them around your neck,
Write them on the tablet of your heart.*
— *Proverbs 3:3 (NKJV)*

See also: James 2:13   James 4:6-7

My mercy is a blanket covering your life.
This mercy of Mine keeps you and envelops you. Recall My mercy, and you will see My love for you.
Mercy covers all your shortcomings and everyone you deal with every day.
Mercy is needed so that you will not be critical. Do not set yourself up as a judge. For I Am Judge.
When you recognize My mercy, you will be able to give it to others.

March 7

Fear and Trembling

> And suddenly, a woman who had a flow of blood for twelve years came from behind and touched the hem of His garment. For she said to herself, "If only I may touch His garment, I shall be made well." But Jesus turned around, and when He saw her He said, "Be of good cheer, daughter; your faith has made you well." And the woman was made well from that hour.
> —Matthew 9:20-22 (NKJV)

She had once been a woman of faith and influence, but now she faced a darkness she could not escape. Doubt pressed in like a weight she could no longer bear. She had prayed, pleaded, and wept until her hope was nearly gone. Even the doctors dismissed her, and despair rose over her mind like a storm. *Where was her God—the One who had done such great miracles?*

Then one day, a whisper reached her heart: *Jesus is healing everyone He touches.* For the first time in years, light flickered within her soul. Yet fear quickly followed—she was forbidden to approach, unclean, unwanted, unseen. Still, something stronger than fear began to rise. She covered her face and slipped quietly into the streets.

She saw the crowd ahead and her heart pounded. There was no way through—so she fell to her knees. Crawling through dust and feet and rejection, she whispered to herself, *"If I can just touch the hem of His garment, I will be healed."*

Her trembling hand reached out. Her fingers brushed the fringe of His robe—and heaven moved. Power surged through her body, washing away years of pain and shame.

Jesus stopped. He turned and called her out before the crowd. Trembling, she stood, her secret now exposed. But when His eyes met hers, love silenced every fear.

Her tears fell freely. The One she had sought had found her.

Now she could say with joy and certainty, *"Jesus is my Healer."*

March 8

Mary, Mary

And she had a sister called Mary, who also sat at Jesus' feet and heard His word.
— *Luke 10:39 (NKJV)*

See also: Luke 8:2   John 20:11-16

I tell you, you are to Me as Mary Magdalene—she who tended to My needs out of a grateful heart, for she was set free from torment and forgiven much. Out of that freedom, she loved deeply and followed Me closely. She stood at My cross, sharing in My agony because her heart belonged wholly to Me. And to her was given the joy of being the first to see Me risen. Her tears of sorrow became tears of inexpressible joy.

So it is with you. Be this Mary to Me.

And what shall I say of the sister of My dear friend Lazarus? Mary sat at My feet, listening intently to every word, her heart longing to know Me. Her desire was met, and so shall yours be. In her grief, I wept with her; then I revealed My glory as she witnessed resurrection life unfold before her eyes. She believed and never doubted. In humility and courage, she anointed My body beforehand, pouring out her love in extravagant worship.

I desire that you be to Me both Marys—one of passionate devotion and one of quiet adoration. Rejoice, for I have raised you up to see Me in resurrection power and to know Me as Life eternal.

Tell others what I reveal to you, and speak of what you have heard from Me. You have been chosen to walk as near to Me as these Marys of Mine.

March 9

Glorious

Arise, shine;
For your light has come!
And the glory of the Lord is risen upon you.
For behold, the darkness shall cover the earth,
And deep darkness the people;
But the Lord will arise over you,
And His glory will be seen upon you.
— *Isaiah 60:1-2 (NKJV)*

See also: Matthew 5:16   John 17:22-23

Contemplation:
Jesus, what is the glory that You spoke of to your disciples?

The Response:
I Am the All-Glorious One. You bear My image. It is My glory that I give to each one who is one with Me. My holiness and honor shine through you, as you reflect My goodness to the world and glorify Me. All that you know has come to you by the illumination of My Spirit. Arise and shine in radiant glory. You are a beacon of light, shining in the darkness. Believe who you are in Me—radiant and glorious, created in My image to reflect My glory.

March 10

Determined

**With my whole heart I have sought You;
Oh, let me not wander from Your commandments!**
— *Psalm 119:10 (NKJV)*

See also: Psalm 143:8   Philippians 3:8   Hebrews 8:9

I Am known by you, for you have sought Me with your whole heart.
Be determined to know Me deeply, for I Am already acquainted with you.
I understand all that you wonder about. Return this kind of intimacy, and let your heart marvel at who I Am.
Think upon My person—I walked the earth as you do.
I have given you My Word and My Spirit so that you may truly know Me.
In My presence you will come to understand Me, and I will transform your thinking.
I will lift you into the realm of My Spirit—where life, freedom, and joy abound,
where condemnation and strife lose their hold.
I Am able to raise you into this newness of life.
Stay close to Me on the path that ascends.
Make it your priority each day to renew your love vows with Me.

March 11

His Delight

**Who forgives all your iniquities,
Who heals all your diseases.**
— *Psalm 103:3 (NKJV)*

See also: James 5:14   Revelation 22:2   Exodus 15:26

When all is well—body and soul—you worship and serve Me out of joy and thankfulness. There are many ways I have provided for your wholeness. Shall I name them?
Obedience to My Word.
Meditation—My Word is medicine to your soul.
Eating the fruits and vegetables I created.
The healing oils found in the leaves.
Worship—for in My presence there is healing.
Purity in body and heart, and the surrender of resentment.
All these I have given for your health and peace. I have also given you My Holy Spirit to fill you with joy and laughter. I Am the One who bears your burdens so that stress and anxiety cannot destroy you. My desire is that you overcome the evils of this world, including sickness.
I Am the Lord who heals you—Yahweh Rapha. How can you doubt, when My very Name declares your healing?

March 12

Take Hold

That you may love the Lord your God, that you may obey His voice, and that you may cling to Him, for He is your life and the length of your days; and that you may dwell in the land which the Lord swore to your fathers, to Abraham, Isaac, and Jacob, to give them.
— Deuteronomy 30:20 (NKJV)

See also: Psalm 119:31   Isaiah 45:5-6

Reach out your hand and take hold of Me. Why the tears?
Take hold of everything that I have given you.
Call to remembrance My goodness in your life.
Clasp tightly the things that I have placed within your reach of faith.
Take hold of My forgiveness, which has included your years of rebellion.
Take hold of My restoration power that has covered your life.
I Am Lord, Restorer, and Healer.
I Am even more to you than this.
I Am Kindness, Goodness, and Mercy.
I glory in those who cling to Me in all that I Am.

March 13

Mind of Christ

Therefore judge nothing before the time, until the Lord comes, who will both bring to light the hidden things of darkness and reveal the counsels of the hearts. Then each one's praise will come from God.
— *1 Corinthians 4:5 (NKJV)*

See also: 1 Corinthians 2:10-16   1 John 2:27

My Word speaks of righteousness.
Therefore, those who teach must be teachers of what is good, pure, and true.
Cling to what is good, and shun all evil in both word and deed.
I will judge the living and the dead by the words that come from their mouths.
Teach the Scriptures, not the doctrines of men.
Teach purity, honor, and unadulterated truth.
Teach all that is right, so that none will go astray.
My Spirit speaks and reveals righteousness to My Body—not judgment or condemnation, for these I reserve for the unbelieving.
I Am the Revealer of the secret aims and purposes of the hearts and minds of men.

March 14

Mercy and Truth

**All the paths of the Lord are mercy and truth,
To such as keep His covenant and His testimonies.**
— Psalm 25:10 (NKJV)

See also: Psalm 85:10   Proverbs 3:3   Matthew 12:7

When you seek to understand My ways, remember that mercy and truth always move together. Without them united, you would misjudge the goodness of who I Am. If you lose sight of all that My mercy holds, doubts of My love would rise to steal the certainty and assurance My Spirit has given you.

Mercy and truth together reveal the higher knowledge of Me. I Am your Father, dealing with you in mercy so that you know the truth—you are forgiven, loved, and blessed. I have prepared you to know Me as merciful, that you may come freely into My presence. I see you through mercy.

Mercy and truth are your right standing with Me, and I preserve you in My mercy. This mercy is new every morning, like the sunrise that announces a fresh beginning for your soul. Mercy goes before truth, and together they reveal who I Am.

March 15

Against the Enemy

> Through the Lord's mercies we are not consumed,
> Because His compassions fail not.
> They are new every morning;
> Great is Your faithfulness.
> — *Lamentations 3:22-23 (NKJV)*

See also: Lamentations 3:33-40   Ephesians 6:13

You need to speak boldly about what I have done for you. This is necessary for overcoming your enemy, Satan. Remember, I give you good things because I Am good. It is My will to bring abundance into your life. I Am kind, merciful, loving, and forgiving. Do not look for Me in evil, or you will find yourself staring into your enemy's eyes.

I do not correct, discipline, or teach through pain, suffering, or hardship. I allow these things, but not for your harm—rather, to strengthen your faith and prepare you for greater blessings ahead. The source of evil is your enemy. I Am Life; the enemy is death.

Pray as I taught you: "Deliver us from evil." Pray with the authority I have given you. "Resist the enemy, and he will flee from you." Many of the ills and circumstances that trouble you will be set right as you obey My Word—pray, resist evil, and fight your battles with truth by refusing to agree with your enemy.

March 16

Be Quiet

Call to Me, and I will answer you, and show you great and mighty things, which you do not know.
— *Jeremiah 33:3 (NKJV)*

See also: Isaiah 30:15

Be quiet, My child, and I will speak.
This day requires your heart and thoughts to be stayed on Me.
Look, I have prepared this day; I walk and talk with you.
Today is ours.
Delight in Me, for you are Mine.
I will be your great reward—the treasure you seek.

March 17

Love Poured Out

"Therefore I say to you, her sins, which are many, are forgiven—for she loved much. But to whom little is forgiven, the same loves little."
— *Luke 7:47 (NKJV)*

See also: Luke 7:37-47

Come into My presence knowing that you are cared for and accepted. Know that you already have My approval and My favor.
Stand in My strength, and be courageous in My love.
Your love for Me has been tightly bottled, kept as something too precious to give—even to Me. But now it is time to break open that love and pour it out at My feet.
Is it costly? Yes. Love always costs something.
Take what you have stored within and, in holy abandonment, pour your love on Me.
Love Me extravagantly, as I have loved you.
Love Me from your heart, beyond the limits of your mind.
Weep if you must—but let your tears fall as worship, and let your love be poured out before Me.

March 18

The Joy of You

These things I have spoken to you, that My joy may remain in you, and that your joy may be full.
—John 15:11 (NKJV)

See also: Acts 2:28

The joy of You is found in lying at Your feet again, willing to be searched by You once more.
This joy comes in listening to Your voice and in knowing Your heart.
There is peace in this abiding.
You have not called Me to chase happiness, but to enter into Your joy.
True joy is not what I receive from You—it is knowing You.
So, Lord, I turn my heart again to rediscover the delight of Your presence, to rest in the sweetness of Your kiss.

March 19

Clothed in Dignity

He has shown you, O man, what is good;
And what does the Lord require of you
But to do justly,
To love mercy,
And to walk humbly with your God?
— *Micah 6:8 (NKJV)*

See also: 2 Corinthians 5:9   Ephesians 1:6   Revelation 3:5

Do not trust in your own evaluations. You cannot see your own nakedness without the help of another. When confronted, do not hide behind feigned modesty. Others may share opinions, but they judge by outward appearances and cannot see as I see.

If you desire to be clothed in beauty, fit for My scrutiny, then accept My opinion. I have shown you how to walk with Me—in humility, love, and mercy. I alone clothe you in robes of white, making you right before Me. I give you beauty so that you will not be found naked but adorned with dignity. Walk carefully before Me, seeking My approval above all. Listen to another's evaluation with an open heart, but always ask Me what I think. Know the true state of your own heart. I Am the One who corrects My children and the One who covers every flaw with mercy and grace.

March 20

Evil Times

Do not say, 'A conspiracy,'
Concerning all that this people call a conspiracy,
Nor be afraid of their threats, nor be troubled.
The Lord of hosts, Him you shall hallow;
Let Him be your fear,
And let Him be your dread.
He will be as a sanctuary,
But a stone of stumbling and a rock of offense
To both the houses of Israel,
As a trap and a snare to the inhabitants of Jerusalem.
— Isaiah 8:12-14 (NKJV)

I Am with you, and I Am for you. Do not fear what others fear or dread. Let Me be your fear and your awe. Do not provoke Me with fear of man or distrust in My goodness.

I Am your sanctuary and your refuge. Fear to offend Me, and trust in Me alone. Others may stumble and fall into the traps of their own reasoning, believing holiness can be achieved by effort. But all who come to My altar are made holy through their consecration to Me.

Look to Me and to My Word. Do not fix your eyes on the distress and darkness around you, for it will cloud your vision. Even in the midst of judgment, watch for the sure promise of My deliverance.

March 21

Beautiful Words

*Then those who feared the LORD spoke to one another,
And the LORD listened and heard them;
So a book of remembrance was written before Him
For those who fear the LORD
And who meditate on His name.
— Malachi 3:16 (NKJV)*

See also: Malachi 3:17

My chosen one, I listen to you from My heart. You were born out of My compassion and mercy. I will lead you with great joy and peace as you make Me your portion in this life. I give you My thoughts and My righteousness as you stand before Me in love.

Know that I Am listening whenever you speak of Me. I Am recording your words in heaven, for I desire to inscribe each one in the Book of Remembrance. Let Me hear your beautiful words.

March 22

Jacob's Blessing

And He said, "Let Me go, for the day breaks."
But he said, "I will not let You go unless You bless me!"
— *Genesis 32:26 (NKJV)*

See also: Genesis 49:22-26   Hebrews 13:20

You have been targeted, attacked, and wounded by the schemes of the enemy. You have been weary and embittered by persecution, yet you have remained strong and steadfast by the Strength that never fails.

Your arms and hands were made strong by Me, the Mighty God of Jacob—by the Names you know Me by: your Shepherd and your Rock. I have helped you even when you did not see it. I will bless you with every promise I have spoken, for all that you need is already found in Me.

In desperation, you cried out, and still you remained with Me despite what your circumstances said. The battle is over. Now you will receive the blessing of Jacob.

March 23

Reconstruction

*For I have eaten ashes like bread,
And mingled my drink with weeping.
— Psalm 102:9 (NKJV)*

See also: Ephesians 2:20-22   Ephesians 3:10   Hebrews 11:10

Today I ask you to look again at the ruins—not to see the ashes, but to see My hand at work in your life. As you look, release all resentment, for I Am and I was in the midst of every broken place. I paid the price for your life, and it will be rebuilt to My honor. I will not fail you.

There is no value in the ashes you have eaten as your bread. Everything has now been exposed in the light of My presence. Arise from the depression where your circumstances have kept you, and rise into a life of praise.

Seek My opinion and listen for My voice. Take to heart the promises of My favor and accept My goodwill in your life. I Am the Builder, and you are My building—dedicated and held together by Love.

March 24

Ask of Heaven

Who redeems your life from destruction,
Who crowns you with lovingkindness and tender mercies,
Who satisfies your mouth with good things,
So that your youth is renewed like the eagle's.
— *Psalm 103:4-5 (NKJV)*

See also: Isaiah 55:11   Isaiah 64:8   Ephesians 2:10

Give Me your reasoning.
Your great need is to yield your will, your mind, and your emotions to Me.
I want to be your God.
Ask Me for what is higher than your thoughts.
Walk with Me in the newness of life.
Surrender all you think you are, and all you think I Am.
When you become a blank canvas, I will paint wonders upon your life, heavenly, good, and glorious things.
These are the things of Me that your mind has not conceived, for you have been concerned with lesser things.
I Am your God.
In humility, give Me all that you are, and I will rebuild all that I Am to you.
My promise is to make you a vessel of honor for My glory.
I ask you to yield to Me and lay everything upon the altar.
You will receive your reward.
You have asked so little of Me.
Ask of Me, ask of heaven.

March 25

Heaviness for Joy

Those who sow in tears
Shall reap in joy.
He who continually goes forth weeping,
Bearing seed for sowing,
Shall doubtless come again with rejoicing,
Bringing his sheaves with him.
— *Psalm 126:5-6 (NKJV)*

See also: Isaiah 12:2-3   Isaiah 51:11   Isaiah 61:3

I direct a willing heart. I also direct the seasons and the times of fulfillment in your life. Let sadness and sorrow fade away. Go forward with joy and singing, bringing in the sheaves.

The highway of holiness is a way of joy; all who walk upon it sing with you. On this highway, there is no sadness—only My joy. I want you to laugh with Me. I Am the One who says to you, "Be filled with joy." You have known enough sorrow in your journey; now walk with Me in gladness.

March 26

Purifying Love

For in Christ Jesus neither circumcision nor uncircumcision avails anything, but faith working through love.
—*Galatians 5:6 (NKJV)*

See also: Song of Songs 8:7

Love is rich, abundant, and free. It consumes your thoughts and brings tears to your eyes. This, My love, moves you so deeply because love is the realization of heaven itself.

Come and place yourself under this flow of love, and out of you will come the newness of life you have longed for. My pure love is the golden oil that feeds the lamp of your spirit and lights it, for love flows from My Spirit.

My love is the flame that burns away the dross, for out of love comes all that is pure. Love has the power to align your thoughts and actions with all that is of heaven, for love is heavenly. In My love, you see rightly, hear rightly, and discern rightly.

The power of love is your greatest treasure.

March 27

God's Family

> I will greatly rejoice in the Lord,
> My soul shall be joyful in my God;
> For He has clothed me with the garments of salvation,
> He has covered me with the robe of righteousness,
> As a bridegroom decks himself with ornaments,
> And as a bride adorns herself with her jewels.
> — *Isaiah 61:10 (NKJV)*

See also: Matthew 12:48-50   John 17:20-26

I have brought you to Myself in and through My very own blood.
I took on your identity to pay the debt you owed.
Now you are Mine.
Wear the robe of righteousness that I have given you.
In this relationship, I say—you are My beloved, and in you I Am well pleased.

March 28

Time Is Rushing In

And do this, knowing the time, that now it is high time to awake out of sleep; for now our salvation is nearer than when we first believed.
— *Romans 13:11 (NKJV)*

Contemplation:
All the time I've wasted—time is running out!

The Response:
Time is not running out; time is rushing in.
Everything is measured by what is eternal.
There will come a day when time is swallowed by eternity,
and time itself will become only a memory.

March 29

Born Royal

> But you are a chosen generation, a royal priesthood, a holy nation, His own special people, that you may proclaim the praises of Him who called you out of darkness into His marvelous light.
> —*1 Peter 2:9 (NKJV)*

See also: Daniel 12:3   Matthew 12:48-50   Luke 19:13

I Am your Father, and My Son is your advocate and friend. You have My Spirit to guide, comfort, and cheer you on at every moment. We are a Royal Family.

You are a celebrated one in My Kingdom, and I want you to know that you are the light shining into the darkness of this world. It is you, My star.

Let My Word parent and delight you daily. You will not become weak in body or soul, for every morning I instruct and encourage you. I Am the great communicator—always available, always speaking.

I love that your joy is to be with Me. You are important in My Kingdom, and I await the moment you step fully into your destiny. Destiny is yours by royal birth. You are to rule and reign with Me.

March 30

Eyes of Love

To the praise of the glory of His grace, by which He made us accepted in the Beloved.
— *Ephesians 1:6 (NKJV)*

See also: Ephesians 2:6   1 Peter 2:9

I see you clothed in My righteousness, as with a robe.
In My presence, you are blameless.
I seat you with Me in heavenly places.
Learn to see with Me from this vantage point.
I see you transferred into My Kingdom of light—
there is no darkness here.
Walk in My light, and others will see Me.
I see you, My Love. I see you, My Bride.
I have betrothed you to Myself with great jealousy.
I see you wearing the crown I have given you.
See yourself seated beside Me, by royal decree.
I see your life as a declaration of all My goodness
and all My faithfulness in your generation.

March 31

Prepare for Eternity

The night is far spent, the day is at hand. Therefore let us cast off the works of darkness, and let us put on the armor of light.
— *Romans 13:12 (NKJV)*

Come and look from above, and you will see the beauty of the earth—and upon it, the battle between good and evil, and the chaos it brings. I Am jealous of My own; this is why you find yourself a foreigner in a strange battleground.

Find your joy in Me. Let Me be your greatest pursuit and satisfaction, for idols will not endure—eternity is approaching. The time has come for the faithful to rise above and take their stand with Me, to be strong and courageous as I have spoken.

Find your joy in Me, for I Am preparing you for eternity.

April 1

Manna for Today

> He had rained down manna on them to eat,
> And given them of the bread of heaven.
> Men ate angels' food;
> He sent them food to the full.
> —Psalm 78:24-25 (NKJV)

See also: John 6:48-51

I Am the Bread that comes from heaven.
Like the manna of old, what you gathered yesterday will not feed your soul today.
My words spoken to you are the manna for this moment.
You cannot store the freshness of My Word, for I supply new provision each day.
Renewal does not come through your understanding, but through the power of fresh revelation found in My words spoken to you.
Come and gather what you need for today—you will find it more than enough.

April 2
Walk in White

Therefore "Come out from among them
And be separate, says the Lord.
Do not touch what is unclean,
And I will receive you."
—*2 Corinthians 6:17 (NKJV)*

See also: Revelation 3:5-6

You are called by My Name, and I have made you worthy.
Separate yourself from all that contaminates your heart and mind.
I Am your great reward when you take pleasure in all that is of Me.
I will give you rest as you purpose in your heart to know Me—more in love than in sacrifice.
Let Me give you My thoughts, and you will be kept in love.
See yourself standing before Me in white,
and let your heart rest in My acceptance.
Walk with Me in white, My Bride.

April 3

All That Hinders

> Do not love the world or the things in the world. If anyone loves the world, the love of the Father is not in him.
> For all that is in the world, the lust of the flesh, the lust of the eyes, and the pride of life, is not of the Father but is of the world.
> — *1 John 2:15–16 (NKJV)*

See also: Matthew 6:33

The world's system has caused many of My own to build layers of protection that keep them from intimacy with Me. What the world esteems—self-reliance, success, knowledge, and the pride of life—has been embraced by My people as necessary for survival. Yet these things keep you from Me, for they keep you from My perfect love.

Even what you consider good is not always necessary. I will strip away, even through adversity, all that the world calls good, that your heart may be revealed before Me.

April 4

By My Spirit

Jesus answered, "Most assuredly, I say to you, unless one is born of water and the Spirit, he cannot enter the kingdom of God. That which is born of the flesh is flesh, and that which is born of the Spirit is spirit. Do not marvel that I said to you, 'You must be born again.'"
—*John 3:5-7 (NKJV)*

See also: Luke 4:18-19   Luke 14:23

I Am the Author and Finisher of Salvation.
My children are born into My Kingdom by My Spirit.
This is not your work, but Mine.
I have only asked you to act as a midwife in the birthing of My own.
Go in My Name, in My authority and power, proclaiming the Good News: salvation has come!
Lift up the cross and proclaim that every offense against Me can and will be forgiven.
The price has been paid, and My Love has been poured out.
Compel them by My love.
I will put My Spirit upon you, anointing you as My chosen vessel.
Do what you see Me do; say what you hear Me say.
Be true, and open your heart.
I will put My words in your mouth and My thoughts in your mind.
I desire children who are born of My Spirit, not of man's methods.

April 5

Heavenly Places

And raised us up together, and made us sit together in the heavenly places in Christ Jesus,
that in the ages to come He might show the exceeding riches of His grace in His kindness toward us in Christ Jesus.
For by grace you have been saved through faith, and that not of yourselves; it is the gift of God, not of works, lest anyone should boast.
For we are His workmanship, created in Christ Jesus for good works, which God prepared beforehand that we should walk in them.
—*Ephesians 2:6-10 (NKJV)*

I will guide you and instruct you as you search for My thoughts.
I go before you as your Captain and your Friend.
Here, as we sit together in My presence, you will come to know My thoughts and the purposes of My heart for you. Together, we sit above—in the heavenly places. I call you to come and sit with Me so that you may experience My favor, My goodness, and My strong love for you.
Here you will find rest from all that weighs you down.
Let My love settle deep within you, and let Me be at home in your heart.
You will know Me through your experience of Me, for love is born in intimacy.
Let My love flood your entire being by faith.
Here, we become One in the Spirit.

April 6

Foundations of Faith

The wind blows where it wishes, and you hear the sound of it, but cannot tell where it comes from and where it goes. So is everyone who is born of the Spirit.
—*John 3:8 (NKJV)*

See also: Hebrews 10:38   Hebrews 11:1-3

Everything that stands has a solid foundation.
Let My Word be that foundation in your life.
Let My words become real to you simply because I have spoken them.
I have given you many precious promises—each one is yours.
Your part is to step into them by faith,
faith that perceives as real what cannot be seen, heard, or touched.
Just as I told Nicodemus, "You cannot see the Spirit, but you can see its effects."
If you struggle to believe, look for the evidence of My Spirit in your life.
You can feel My presence and know Me by the experience of My Spirit.
You can see the effects of My power working within you.
Believe Me when I say that faith makes real the unseen—
things that were not come into being through faith.
When you stand in this kind of faith, I Am well pleased,
for it is My Word you are believing in.

April 7

Hopeful Expectation

And now, Lord, what do I wait for?
My hope is in You.
—Psalm 39:7 (NKJV)

See also: Psalm 146:5 Jeremiah 29:11 Romans 5:5 Hebrews 6:18-19

I Am in the midst of every trial, sickness, and adversity—working on your behalf.
Put your faith in Me by placing your hope in Me.
There are three foundations for walking with Me in victory: Faith, Hope, and Love.
I have surrounded Hope with Faith and Love, and Hope stands in the middle for a reason.
As you practice faith in Me, Hope will rise and lead you into My Love.
Hope is essential, for without it you might believe the lie of the enemy—that I Am against you in adversity.
But Hope, the confident expectation of My goodness in your life, gives you great advantage.
Hope is the anchor of your mind, will, and emotions.
This anchor, called Hope, carries you beyond the storm and into the calm harbor where I Am.
Find Hope, and you will find Me.

April 8

Goldfish

**That there should be no schism in the body, but that the members should have the same care for one another.
And if one member suffers, all the members suffer with it; or if one member is honored, all the members rejoice with it.
Now you are the body of Christ, and members individually.**
—1 Corinthians 12:25-27 (NKJV)

See also: Philippians 2:2-4

I see many of My children trapped like goldfish in glass bowls—always waiting to be fed, coming to the surface for air, and watching others look in on them. Their condition never changes. They grow, yet never swim beyond their limited view.
Do you see them? Trapped as they are, you were once one of them.
Goldfish are so dependent on their environment that they do not see the limits keeping them confined.
They look at others as "not in the bowl," when I meant for them to live outside—fishing and catching souls in My Name.
I want every "glass bowl" emptied into the ocean of My love,
where there are no limits set by the opinions of men;
where the Bread of Heaven is their daily provision,
and where My Spirit is the very air they breathe.
I Am freeing My people from all that binds them to sameness.
I desire children who love one another with My love.
Go—empty the goldfish bowls with this truth.

April 9

Four Women

> And Joshua spared Rahab the harlot, her father's household, and all that she had. So she dwells in Israel to this day, because she hid the messengers whom Joshua sent to spy out Jericho.
> —*Joshua 6:25 (NKJV)*

See also: Genesis 38:11-26   Ruth 1:11-18   2 Samuel 12:24-25

I chose four desperate women who, in the face of death, turned to Me.
They did not blame Me, nor believe their circumstances were beyond My repair.
Tamar was disappointed in marriage and grieved the loss of her husband and her inheritance.
I stood with her as she confronted betrayal to preserve the lineage of Judah.
Rahab chose life when she recognized My power to deliver.
I established her in My household as a sign to all who risk everything to follow Me.
Ruth knew love and loss. Yet what she saw in her mother-in-law awakened faith in her heart.
She left her homeland to follow after Me. I became her Redeemer, covering her under the shadow of My wing.
I gave her the desire of her heart—to become a bride and a mother.
Her son, by My decree, was placed in the house of David.
Bathsheba was taken from her home by the desire of a king and bore the weight of shame.
She mourned the death of her husband and her firstborn son, yet refused bitterness.
After the birth of her second son, I spoke to her:
"I call this son Jedidiah, for I love him."
From her sorrow, I raised up Solomon—heir to the throne of David.
These four women declare My power to redeem and restore.
They proclaim that what seems dead will live again.

April 10

Knowing Me

Deep calls unto deep at the noise of Your waterfalls;
All Your waves and billows have gone over me.
—*Psalm 42:7 (NKJV)*

See also: Matthew 11:27   John 3:5-6   1 Corinthians 2:9-12

You can learn of Me,
but will you truly know Me apart from My Spirit?
Deep calls to deep.
Only the mind open to My Spirit can receive divine revelation from the Spirit of Truth.
I have told you that I sent My Spirit to do this for you.
My Spirit takes Truth and makes it the very words of life within you.
I Am in close fellowship with you by My Spirit.
He draws from the throne room of the Father
and imparts to you everything that is of Me.
Everything I desire to reveal, I disclose to those who are Mine.
It is My Spirit who brings life and revelation from My Word.
Those who believe and trust Me in this will have the mind of Christ
and move beyond mere intellectual knowledge.

April 11

Seeking His Face

*My soul longs, yes, even faints
For the courts of the Lord;
My heart and my flesh cry out for the living God.*
—*Psalm 84:2 (NKJV)*

See also: John 12:21

Lay hold of the doors of heaven and call out to Me.
Be relentless in your pursuit of Me.
I will open to those who will not stop seeking Me.
Say to Me, "I must see Jesus!"
I will come to you and fill your heart with the hope and joy of My glory.
When you feel estranged, seek My face.
Wait at the gates of heaven in your longing for Me until I come to you.
I will reveal Myself to you, for I never forsake My lovers.
Stay until I come.

April 12
Faith and Sacrifice

Then the king said to Araunah, "No, but I will surely buy it from you for a price; nor will I offer burnt offerings to the Lord my God with that which costs me nothing."
So David bought the threshing floor and the oxen for fifty shekels of silver.
—*2 Samuel 24:24 (NKJV)*

See also: Matthew 6:19-21 Luke 12:19-20

Contemplation:
What is a faith offering?

The Response:
Offer to Me that which costs you.
When I stir your heart to give, let faith arise.
I desire to free you from anything that would possess your heart.
Let go of what binds you.
Let what you value remain Mine.
Offer to Me your sacrifice, mixed with faith, and I will reward you.

April 13

The Veil

Behold, you are fair, my love!
Behold, you are fair!
You have dove's eyes behind your veil.
Your hair is like a flock of goats,
Going down from Mount Gilead.
—*Song of Songs 4:1 (NKJV)*

See also: Mark 15:38   Hebrews 9:3-8   Hebrews 10:19

I have torn the veil in two from top to bottom.
Nothing can separate you from My presence now.
I reveal Myself to you as your betrothed Husband.
Stay with Me and do not leave this place.
I part your veil to place a kiss upon your forehead.
Keep searching for My face, past every veil that remains between us.
Your one need is My nearness; your spirit needs Mine.
My Bride, anticipate Me lifting the veil from your face.

April 14

The Sparrow

> **Even the sparrow has found a home, and the swallow a nest for herself, where she may lay her young— even Your altars, O Lord of hosts, My King and my God.**
> — *Psalm 84:3 (NKJV)*

Like a sparrow returning to its nest—oh, how My heart is pleased!
I have placed you near My altar, where My presence dwells, to nurture others and be nurtured.
Here you have found a place of rest, and your heart is happy.
It is My presence you love and have returned to,
not by your own will, but by My choosing.
Once again, I have laid My hand upon you.
So sing—sing all day long!
Here you will stay because of your great desire,
a desire I Myself will fan into a bright flame of fire.
All who dwell in My presence are happy.
Now be blessed.

April 15

A Prepared Place

*In My Father's house are many mansions; if it were not so, I would have told you. I go to prepare a place for you.
And if I go and prepare a place for you, I will come again and receive you to Myself; that where I am, there you may be also.*
—*John 14:2-3 (NKJV)*

I Am eternal, not marked by time.
This space for us is an eternal reality—a place prepared for you to come, arriving and returning as often as you desire.
I Am always ready to meet with you in this heavenly realm.
You have waited long enough.
I prepared this way for us when the veil was torn in two.
This is the way I spoke of to My disciples—you know it, for I Am the Way.
Where I Am, you may come and be with Me.
I would have you never leave this space.
Dwell with Me here, and your eyes will see, your ears will hear, as I reveal Myself to you.
Wait no longer for heaven's reality!
I Am closer to you than you know.
Heaven becomes real as you live in this truth:
I have prepared the way for you to be alone with Me—now and forever.

April 16

King's Daughter

> Listen, O daughter,
> Consider and incline your ear;
> Forget your own people also,
> And your father's house;
> So the King will greatly desire your beauty;
> Because He is your Lord, worship Him.
> And the daughter of Tyre will come with a gift;
> The rich among the people will seek your favor.
> The royal daughter is all glorious within the palace;
> Her clothing is woven with gold.
> She shall be brought to the King in robes of many colors;
> The virgins, her companions who follow her, shall be brought to You.
> —*Psalm 45:10-14 (NKJV)*

See also: Song of Songs 2-6

You are My daughter, and My beauty rests upon you.
Let My beauty and love make you courageous.
You were brought to Me in love—so let that same love protect, comfort, and sustain you.
Yes, be sustained by My love.
Feel My hand embrace you.
Be My companion as we climb the rocky, steep places of life.
Let Me hide you in the sheltered place where I Am.
There you will hear My voice and touch My face.
Be My royal daughter, all glorious within.
You are in My Kingdom.
Reign with Me.

April 17

My Sheep

My sheep hear My voice, and I know them, and they follow Me.
—John 10:27 (NKJV)

My heart longs for you, as your soul longs for Me.
I Am your Good Shepherd.
I watch over you and care for you daily, guiding you to pastures I have prepared for you.
I Am the voice of Truth.
You will find that My voice is your confidence and joy—there is no soundness in any other voice.
Listen for it.
I will comfort you and cause you to rest in peace.
Enjoy the sweet fellowship I have made ready for you
as you walk and talk with Me each day.

April 18

Keep Your Heart

Keep your heart with all diligence, for out of it spring the issues of life.
—*Proverbs 4:23 (NKJV)*

See also: Titus 1:15 James 3:17

To the pure, all things are pure.
Keep your heart in My love.
My desire is to purify your life through love.
Surrender all your doubts and fears to Me.
Keep your heart open.

April 19

Unlock Your Heart

And we have known and believed the love that God has for us. God is love, and he who abides in love abides in God, and God in him.
—1 John 4:16 (NKJV)

See also: John 15:4-11, John 17:21-22

You need to have confidence in Me, and let your heart take courage in times of frustration, trial, and distress.
I have already deprived the enemy of his power to harm you.
Now is the time to unlock your heart.
I want to take My rightful place as your Shield and your protection.
How can you deny Me the deepest part of your heart when you are asking Me to come near?
I Am here—closer than you know.
I Am your very breath, yet you do not always discern it, for your heart stands guarded.
Have I not said that My dwelling is within your heart?
Take down the walls you have built, and you will realize how near I Am.
I do not come and go—I Am here, and I remain.
I long for you to know that My residence is in you.
You are made full and complete in this living, experiential knowledge.
This awareness of My constant nearness is My delight, My joy, My gladness, and My desire.

April 20

Promised Rain

And said to his servant, "Go up now, look toward the sea."
So he went up and looked, and said, "There is nothing."
And seven times he said, "Go again."
Then it came to pass the seventh time, that he said, "There is a cloud, as small as a man's hand, rising out of the sea!" So he said, "Go up, say to Ahab, 'Prepare your chariot, and go down before the rain stops you.'"
Now it happened in the meantime that the sky became black with clouds and wind, and there was a heavy rain. So Ahab rode away and went to Jezreel.
—1 Kings 18:43-45 (NKJV)

See also: Hosea 6:1-3 Zecheriah 10:1

Your waiting prepares the dry ground to receive all that I have promised you.
I come as the latter rain—to water the dry and thirsty soil that holds the seeds of your faith.
I promise to come to you as you wait on Me.
I promise to heal and revive your life.
I will restore you, bind up your wounds, and make a way for you to live before Me in love.
I desire your love, not your sacrifice.
Wait with expectancy, looking for even the smallest cloud.
You will receive the blessing that pours down from Me in due time.
Look in anticipation—rain is coming!
You will not be destroyed.
I Am the Fountain of Living Waters, and I will pour out upon you as you thirst for Me.
Cry out, "Rain is on the way!"

April 21

Renewal

*Therefore we do not lose heart, even though our outward man is perishing,
yet the inward man is being renewed day by day.
For our light affliction, which is but for a moment, is working for us a far
more exceeding and eternal weight of glory,
while we do not look at the things which are seen, but at the
things which are not seen.
For the things which are seen are temporary, but the things which are
not seen are eternal.*
—*2 Corinthians 4:16-18 (NKJV)*

Let Me renew your mind each day, and you will find the strength to carry on.
Trust Me in these days of distress.
Look with Me toward all that is eternal, and let My love sustain you.
I Am preparing you for more than you know.
This transformation will surprise you.
Take courage, and let hope arise.

April 22

Ark of God

There I will meet with you, and I will commune with you from above the mercy seat, from between the two cherubim which are upon the ark of the Testimony, of all things which I will give you in commandment unto the children of Israel.
—*Exodus 25:22 (NKJV)*

See also: 1 Samuel 4:5-7

I have placed My glory within you to be carried into the darkness of the battlefield. In you is a deposit of My glory to reveal who I Am to others. Do not think this is a hard thing, for it is simply allowing Me to remain in you in My fullness.

Remember the mercy seat where I meet with you daily, and the covenant of the blood of Jesus sprinkled there for your sanctification. You carry My glory with you. Like the Ark, you go forth from My presence, and everywhere your foot touches, I hallow the ground.

Know that what you carry is priceless, powerful, and beautiful to behold. It is the gold of heaven made visible on earth through you, the one who bears My glory. Do not discount your frail vessel, for within you I have placed My glory and My power. The earth will tremble as you come to know what you carry.

April 23

My Story, My Song

**You number my wanderings;
Put my tears into Your bottle;
Are they not in Your book?**
—*Psalm 56:8 (NKJV)*

Today I want to say thank You for all You have done in my life. When I open the story of my journey, I see the pain, tears, and disappointment fade away in the wonder of all that You are.

Without You, the book of my life would have been too long and cruel. But You have written over every page with Your mercy. Now my life reads like poetry, echoing the sound of Your love.

"This is my story, this is my song,
praising my Savior all the day long."

You have rewritten the story of my life and turned it into a beautiful book of poems and songs of love—sung by angels above.

April 24
With Me

*But let all those who put their trust in You rejoice,
Let them ever shout for joy, because You defend them,
Let those also who love Your name be joyful in You.
—Psalm 5:11 (NKJV)*

See also: Psalm 35:9   Matthew 26:36-41

Pray with Me
Pray with Me. I tell you, I will aid all who persevere in faith without wavering.
Then arise from your circumstances, knowing that I Am your very life.
Let your confidence in Me shine, and I will clothe you with My glory.

Stay with Me
Stay with Me, as in the garden—with tears—until I send you relief.
Do not leave until you sense My presence has come.
Follow Me, even into the night of great trouble, and remain by My side.
Do not lose heart, nor become fearful and give up.

Play with Me
Be joyful in all that I have given you.
Remember the many times I have rescued and delivered you,
and let these become signposts for your future.
I delight in a joyful, trusting child.

April 25

Love of God

Many, O Lord my God, are Your wonderful works which You have done; and Your thoughts toward us cannot be recounted to You in order. If I would declare and speak of them, they are more than can be numbered.
—*Psalm 40:5 (NKJV)*

See also: Psalm 139:1-18   Song of Songs 8:6

Contemplation:
Can I really know Your love?

The Response:
How is it that you wrestle with My great love?
Ask for My Spirit to fill the empty places in your heart.
When you lie down, feel My love covering you.
When you rise, let My thoughts of you fill your mind—for I think of you more often than you think of yourself.
Let these thoughts sink deep into your heart.
When misery comes, worship Me, and I will comfort you with My love.
Live today in My love, and you will find the joy and strength to go on.

April 26

Obedience Is...

I beseech you therefore, brethren, by the mercies of God, that you present your bodies a living sacrifice, holy, acceptable to God, *which is* your reasonable service.
—*Romans 12:1 (NKJV)*

See also: Job 36:11

Obedience is a maturity, a coming of age, a settledness that becomes a place of security.
It is a willingness to remain childlike and trust the path He chooses.
It is the place where you believe He is able, and you release your need to control.
It is the desire for more of God in your life and the offering of yourself to Christ.

April 27

Getaway

**The Lord also will be a refuge for the oppressed,
A refuge in times of trouble.**
—*Psalm 9:9 (NKJV)*

See also: Psalm 46:7-11   Psalm 91:1-10

There is a place that only I know, where you and I may flee. Come away with Me to this place of complete safety. Here you will find peace and protection. In the secret place, nothing can harm you, for the accuser does not dare to come, nor does he know the way. Here, in this place, you are under the wings of the Almighty, where no fear abides, for I Am around and over you. Hurry away to this place where all evil fades. Here is a sanctuary for the weary, the torn, and the accused. You will experience My love and peace in this getaway.

April 28

I Will Worship

"But the hour is coming, and now is, when the true worshipers will worship the Father in spirit and truth; for the Father is seeking such to worship Him. God is Spirit, and those who worship Him must worship in spirit and truth."
— *John 4:23–24 (NKJV)*

See also: Zephaniah 3:17

I sing over you with joy! In extravagant worship, My love for you is revealed. Let your worship rise from deep within you—up to Me, where it is amplified! Deep calls to deep, My Spirit to yours. So pour out your worship, taking every opportunity to surrender completely, holding nothing back.
Behold, I come to you in the reality your soul longs for. In true worship, I Am seen, and I Am known by you as I reveal Myself. Heaven opens for you when you look beyond earthly things and see My majesty.
If you desire to have more of Me, then withhold nothing in worship.

April 29

Weakness to Strength

And why do you look at the speck in your brother's eye, but do not consider the plank in your own eye?
—*Matthew 7:3 (NKJV)*

See also: John 21:22   Romans 16:20   Ephesians 6:10-17

When you are always looking to "see" the weaknesses of others, you become blind to your own. When opposition comes, check your thoughts and your heart with Me. See what I Am doing in your life.

Remember, do not judge according to the flesh, for flesh and blood is not the realm where you fight the enemy. The battle you are in is spiritual.

Look for the ways of peace, and you will stand on Satan's head. Your one need is for My approval.

Do not look at another's path and compare yourself. What is that to you? You follow Me.

I will use every weakness in your life to reveal My strength.

April 30

The Flame

For the LORD your God is a consuming fire, a jealous God.
—Deuteronomy 4:24 (NKJV)

See also: Song Of Songs 8:6   Matthew 3:11

I Am a jealous God and therefore a consuming fire. Do not disregard My longing for your attention by thinking of Me as anything less than a fire that burns for you every day. Fan the flame of your love for Me in remembrance of My jealous love over you.

I Am the Refiner's fire. I Am still the same, for out of the fire I spoke to Moses, and out of the fire of My Word I have spoken to you, My disciple. Fan the flame of My passion as you recall all the words I have spoken to your heart and mind.

You are Mine, and My desire is to cast fire upon the earth through your passion for Me. I look for you to carry the flame born out of My very words spoken to you.

All That I Am

May

May 1

In Strength

The Lord is my strength and song, And He has become my salvation; He is my God, and I will praise Him; My father's God, and I will exalt Him.
—*Exodus 15:2 (NKJV)*

See also: Psalm 18:2   Psalm 46:10   Psalm 144:2

Let your soul know Who I Am.
I Am the Rock upon which you stand.
I Am lifting you up and holding your hand.
I Am your strength.
In My love, steadfast, remain.
I AM the Fortress and your High Tower.
Look up from your valley, come up to the hills.
Look down to see all beneath your feet.
Trust Me and do not strive.
All is subdued from the heights.
In My strength rejoice and be still.

May 2

Five Stones

> Then David said to the Philistine, "You come to me with a sword, and with a spear, and with a shield, but I come to you in the name of the LORD of hosts, the God of the armies of Israel, whom you have defied."
> —*1 Samuel 17:45 (NKJV)*
>
> See also: 1 Samuel 16 & 17

I chose David, overlooked and seen as insignificant, to be anointed by Me. He was My choice to deliver Israel from fear and torment. I gave David My Spirit, and he became strong in Me. He was unafraid to face anything that threatened him or the sheep in his care, for he knew that My power was in him.

David had a testimony with Me. In My faithfulness, he saw his enemy as a fallen foe. With five chosen stones, he felled the giant that caused fear. The first was the **stone of Faith**, carried by My Spirit to hit the target I intended. The second was **Confidence**, for he trusted in My ability to save. The third was **Lordship**, for every battle belongs to Me. The fourth was **No Fear**, for David allowed no fear of man or enemy to oppose his faith. The fifth was **The Word**, for he knew My Word and trusted it to defeat the enemy.

My Word is the sword you use to cut off your enemy's head and win every battle. Run headlong into your fight—I Am the Lord, mighty to save and deliver you with just one stone.

May 3

A Friend Loves

A friend loves at all times, And a brother is born for adversity.
—Proverbs 17:17 (NKJV)

See also: 1 Samuel 18:1-3   Hebrews 10:24

Your companionship is invigorating! In love and joy, we have shared victories won through our Savior's mercy. We take communion together, basking in His love. We spur one another on to ask for more and to become more in His Kingdom. We speak of His greatness and His leading in our lives. With His love within us, we are knitted together. As Jonathan and David were, so we are one—loving each other with the Savior's love, till death do us part.

May 4

The Trumpet Call

*So Jesus said to them, "Because of your unbelief, for
assuredly, I say to you,
if you have faith as a mustard seed, you will say to this mountain,
'Move from here to there,' and it will move, and nothing will be
impossible for you."*
—Matthew 17:20 (NKJV)

See also: John 6:2-16   Judges 7:8-20   Zechariah 4:6

The trumpets of Jericho are being found by My Joshuas and My Gideons, who are rallying all who will believe Me. They are crying out, "Who will go in faith to march around the impossible walls—the walls of pride, arrogance, and affluence; the walls of unbelief? These are the walls of the great city of Jericho where I Am not found."
Find the trumpet of My voice, you who believe Me, for you are My Joshuas. These walls will break by the sound of My Spirit's voice. I will be found again by those who have hidden behind the walls of disbelief. The city's walls will fall, and from America's shores, My victory will resound. The foundations of hell will shake open, and the heavens will be revealed. My victory will be made known once again—for the battle is Mine.

May 5

Delight Yourself in the Lord

The steps of a good man are ordered by the Lord, and He delights in his way.
—Psalm 37:23 (NKJV)

See also: Exodus 33:11   2 Peter 1:19-21

You are My Joshua. I have chosen you because you know My presence. You are to lead others in My strength. I have placed My desires within you for My purposes. Walk with Me in faith as I give you the desires of your heart.

Do not look to the right or to the left—only to the path I have set before you. Believe every promise I have spoken. By faith, you will lead others into the same freedom that has been given to you. Keep every prophetic word deep within your heart. I desire to see My Kingdom advance, for it is alive and moves at My command. Your part is to behold the great things I will do—these are the greater works promised to those who believe. Check your heart often.

May 6

Lollipops

Oh, taste and see that the Lord is good; Blessed is the man who trusts in Him!
—Psalm 34:8 (NKJV)

See also: Psalm 119:103   Jeremiah 15:16

My eternal goodness, when taken and enjoyed, is like lollipops from heaven—gifts from Me to you. When you recognize My goodness over your life, it will free you from the lies of the enemy. That is why I said, "Taste and see that the Lord is good."

I want you to enjoy all that I give you from above, even My very Word. My Word is not only for instruction and correction, but also for your delight. Every word is written by My Spirit in love. When you regard My words as sweet treats from heaven, you will taste My goodness in your life.

Let My Word stay on your tongue and in your mouth. Do not merely take a bite or devour it quickly. Be My true child—one who knows how to savor every sweet thing I give. Take time to enjoy the beauty, color, and flavor of every word I have spoken to you. Let your heart and mind remain in My Word long enough to draw out its sweetness, and you will come to know My goodness deeply.

I have given you many lollipops—surprisingly colored treats from My heart to yours. Pass some out to others who need a taste of My goodness.

May 7

The Blood

How much more shall the blood of Christ, who through the eternal Spirit offered Himself without spot to God, cleanse your conscience from dead works to serve the living God?
—*Hebrews 9:14 (NKJV)*

See also: Hebrews 13:20   John 6:55-56   1 John 5:6

My blood was shed to bring you My very life and restore dominion to you. This is the agreement of heaven—the blood, the water, and the Spirit. My life is in you, My beloved.

You were born from My side at the cross, when My heart burst open for you. The water and blood that flowed forth carried the power of new life. You were taken from My side to live by My side, as My Bride.

I have given you the power of My life, for My blood flows through your veins. Apply My blood over your mind, your identity, and every circumstance. Lay your hands on others and declare the power of My blood to heal, restore, and set them free.

Live in the covenant of My blood, and walk boldly in the power I have given you.

May 8

Raining Flowers

He shall come down like rain upon the grass before mowing, Like showers that water the earth.
—*Psalm 72:6 (NKJV)*

See also: Hosea 6:3   Acts 14:17

It's raining flowers!
It's My goodness, My love coming down in showers from heaven above.
Rain falls onto a parched land. The shower of My blessing that restores and refreshes the flowers from My hand.
Look up, it's raining flowers to restore the dry places. It's My love, My goodness, My hope on their faces.

May 9

Lion of Judah

> The scepter shall not depart from Judah, Nor a lawgiver
> from between his feet,
> Until Shiloh comes; And to Him shall be the obedience of the people.
> —*Genesis 49:10 (NKJV)*

See also: 1 Timothy 1:17   Revelation 5:5   Revelation 17:14

See, I stand behind you as the Lion of Judah—strong and mighty. What do you fear? Nothing shall harm those who sit with Me and know Me as I Am, the conquering King who has already won the victory over Satan.

Those who trust in Me are ruled by My love. Come into My court and sit calmly at My feet, knowing Me as the One who has triumphed. There is joy, peace, and power in believing in Me as your conquering King.

To those who know Me as I Am, I give the victor's crown. Wear it and trust in the Lion of Judah, who watches over His own. I will raise up all who see Me as the Lion to rule with Me.

May 10

Be Me

"A disciple is not above his teacher, nor a servant above his master.
It is enough for a disciple that he be like his teacher, and a servant like his master.
If they have called the master of the house Beelzebub, how much more will they call those of his household!
Therefore do not fear them. For there is nothing covered that will not be revealed, and hidden that will not be known."
—*Matthew 10:24-26 (NKJV)*

See also: Matthew 16:19   Luke 12:32

These are the days I told you about. Men will love themselves rather than Me. They will be content with their own understanding, relying on intellect instead of revelation. A mind not surrendered to My Spirit will always stir up discord—whether inwardly or against others.

Take pity on some and have mercy on others. Be unmovable, fearing nothing except to displease Me. I have already told you of persecution—embrace it with My power within you and My joy in your heart. We are one in this endeavor.

When you look into the face of the accuser, what do you see? If it is not love, joy, or peace, it is because they lack the very thing they long for. Smile and be happy! Be like your Master.

May 11

The Train

> Then the LORD said to me, 'Arise, begin *your* journey before the people, that they may go in and possess the land which I swore to their fathers to give them.'
> —*Deuteronomy 10:11 (NKJV)*

The train is ready for boarding, and your ticket marked "**MORE**" has been placed in your hand. You can redeem it anytime you need—just hold on to it. Do not hesitate to take your seat on this train called "**ARISE**," for it's heading in the opposite direction of the world.

There are no seats labeled *doubt* or *disbelief*. I Am directing your journey, and your seat is right beside Me. I Am your Father, and you will marvel at My goodness. Stay on board at every stop, and don't get off unless I tell you. Expect great things every day!

May 12

Create With Me

So God created man in His own image; in the image of God He created him; male and female He created them.
—*Genesis 1:27 (NKJV)*

See also: Ezekiel 36:26-27

You create by My light, for I have made you in My image.
When you learn to see value as I see it, you will create with Me.
Do not worry about perfection, for the image itself will speak for Me—even a thousand words. Be diligent to perfect the gift, but do not let perfection rise up against the need. Show the world who I Am and what I long to say through the gift I have placed in you.
I love every created thing! What I have placed within you is precious to Me. The art you create will hang upon hearts and be reproduced in the minds of others. Give back to Me what I have planted in you, and see what I will do.
See with the eyes of your heart what I wish to say through one image. Watch My Word become visible upon the surface of your canvas. Display what I long to speak in this time. Words may pass quickly by another's heart, but an image created by Me will ignite a flame.

May 13

Past the Gates of Praise

Give unto the Lord the glory due to His name; Worship the Lord in the beauty of holiness.
—Psalm 29:2 (NKJV)

See also: Psalm 95:6   John 4:23

The gate of worship lies beyond the gates of praise, for in worship the reality of heaven is revealed. Go past the gates of praise—lay down your pride and enter into true worship.

In worship, the flame of your passion for Me is ignited. I dwell in this holy place where you may enter and be set free from all earthly ties. Offer yourself to Me as a living sacrifice, and you will experience the fullness of true worship and share in My joy.

I have called you to worship Me by stepping into the unseen waters—to dance before Me without fear. I desire a carefree Bride, one who is self-abandoned in true worship. Come and give to Me the worship that I have placed deep within you.

May 14

Set Free

Therefore if the Son makes you free, you shall be free indeed.
—*John 8:36 (NKJV)*

See also: Galatians 4:31

Know that I lead you in a way that is not hard. I go before you, for I Am the Way. All I ask is that you surrender everything to Me. I want you to be free—free to walk in the liberty of My Spirit.

Listen to Me when I say this: you have made the easy hard by your own thinking. My way is easy, and My burden is light. Rest in Me, and I will take your hand and cause you to rise in newness of life—free from self-criticism.

This is the day of freedom! Say with Me now, "The chains are broken; the burdens lifted!" Trust Me. Give Me your heart in gratitude for all that I Am doing. I Am your gentle Deliverer, standing guard over you from all that comes against you.

May 15

Destiny

When my father and my mother forsake me, Then the Lord will take care of me.
—*Psalm 27:10 (NKJV)*

See also: 1 Corinthians 1:8   2 Corinthians 1:22   Ephesians 1:13-14

You are blessed in your knowledge of Me as Father.
I look at you and see you as My blameless child—one who brings Me praise as you allow Me to love you.
Daily, I deliver you from all your shortcomings and failures because I Am good. Live in the truth that you, My child, are stamped with My approval and favor. You are sealed with My Holy Spirit to live and shine in these days. It is My good pleasure to reveal My purposes to you and to work out My plans until I return. Know that your life brings Me honor and glory!

May 16

As Esther

> The king loved Esther more than all the other women, and she obtained grace and favor in his sight more than all the virgins; so he set the royal crown upon her head and made her queen instead of Vashti.
> —*Esther 2:17 (NKJV)*

See also: Esther 3:8   Esther 5:2

I am clothed in royal apparel, and You have set a crown upon my head in Your Kingdom. I have You to run to when Your Name and authority are challenged. I will bow to You alone and will not regard those who stand in opposition to Your laws and thoughts.

You are King, and Your thoughts are higher—often misunderstood by a world eager to cast off Your authority and silence Your people through its decrees. Now is the time to fast and pray. I will wait and pray. My King will hold out His scepter to me and grant my request, my petition, as I wait for His perfect timing.

May 17

The Adventure

> But Ruth said: 'Entreat me not to leave you, Or to turn back from following after you; For wherever you go, I will go; And wherever you lodge, I will lodge; Your people shall be my people, And your God, my God.'
> —*Ruth 1:16 (NKJV)*
>
> See also: Acts 9:15

I have called you into an adventure with Me. It is time to leave comfort behind and look ahead to what is possible. The world seeks security in routine and finds assurance in illusions of its own making. But I Am always moving you into new places that can only be found in Me.

Faith calls you to leave the temporary and live for the eternal. This is what faith looks like—complete trust in Me. Welcome to the great adventure!

May 18

Heavenly Places

That in the ages to come He might show the exceeding riches of His grace in His kindness toward us in Christ Jesus.
—*Ephesians 2:7 (NKJV)*

See also: Ephesians 6:7   Hebrews 10:22

You know Me. I Am your Captain and your Friend.
When you draw near to My Presence, you can know My thoughts, feel My heart, and understand the purposes I have for you. Together—Me in you, and you in Me—we are raised up to sit in the heavenly realm with My Father. Out of My kindness, I call you to come and sit. My favor and goodness are yours to experience. My strong love surrounds you, giving you rest from all that has held you down.

May 19

The Chalice

> For this is My blood of the new covenant, which is shed for many for the remission of sins.
> —*Matthew 26:28 (NKJV)*

See also: Luke 22:20   John 21:20   1 Corinthians 3:16   Philippians 3:10

Contemplation:
"What does fellowship with Me look like?"

The Response:
My fellowship is like a chalice—beautiful and ornate—for it holds the blood of the New Covenant and the invitation to My table. See the cup in all its beauty, even the cup of Elijah that was present the night My disciples ate with Me. This is the cup of all that is new, brought into being by the blood of the Lamb.

The cup of My blood, poured out for you, is the forgiveness that makes our fellowship possible. In this cup is the communion of the Father, the Son, and the Holy Spirit. My Passover was established as a memorial forever. You must be under the blood of the Lamb for Me to pass over your sins—only then can true communion exist between us.

You are the dwelling place of My Spirit, and this blood covers the door of your heart. Sit at My table and partake of the cup of fellowship with Me. Break the Bread of Life together and drink the fellowship of My suffering—being conformed to My death. Be like John in love and closeness to Me; rest your head upon My chest.

May 20

In Suffering

The righteous cry out, and the Lord hears, And delivers them out
of all their troubles.
The Lord is near to those who have a broken heart, And saves such as
have a contrite spirit.
Many are the afflictions of the righteous, But the Lord delivers
him out of them all.
—*Psalm 34:17-19 (NKJV)*

See also: Psalm 39:7   Psalm 118:14   1 John 5:4-5

You may pour out your grief to Me, but remember—I have already provided all you need in Christ Jesus. Worship Me, for worship is necessary in your trial. I will be your help when you stop searching for escape and cease relying on your own wisdom.

The kind friends I have given you are My blessing to you now. They will strengthen you in your faithfulness to Me. You are not a victim of these circumstances, for I Am on your side.

Your life here is brief compared to eternity, to the glory and the reward that await you. You are important to Me! Have I not visited you every morning? I Am your Keeper. I Am merciful, and I Am listening. Do not let the Adversary overwhelm you.

May 21

Love and Honor

But above all these things put on love, which is the bond of perfection.
—Colossians 3:14 (NKJV)

See also: I Corinthians 12:7-12

Give Me all the opinions you hold of yourself, and look instead to the faith I have given you. Measure yourself by this faith alone.

You are connected to the members I have placed around you. This Body depends upon Me—and upon each other. I have given gifts and talents to all so they may be used for My glory.

Prophecy has been given to those near you to help answer your longing for this gift. Learn from Me and trust Me. Do not look around for the opinions of others regarding My work in your life. Marvel at what I Am doing, and at My great love for you.

May 22

My Word

Sanctify them by Your truth. Your word is truth.
—John 17:17 (NKJV)

See also: Hebrews 1:2

My Word gives you examples of how to conduct yourself. The sum of My Word is truth. To the weak and downcast, I speak through My Psalms and the songs of David. To those who stray, I have given examples so that My Church would not repeat their errors. To My Church, I have given clear instructions on how it is to be governed, so that there may be unity among you.

In these last days, I have spoken to you through My Son. Be sure that you know well what I have said, for I will judge all things by the authority of My Word. Let My Word bring you light in darkness and confidence in trial. My Word is the compass that points you true north so that you will not lose your way.

May 23

Victorious One

Peter, seeing him, said to Jesus, 'But Lord, what about this man?'
—*John 21:21 (NKJV)*

See also: 2 Corinthians 13:4   Hebrews 12:3-4

"Follow Me!"
I go before you in pain and in suffering. Follow Me, and you will be victorious, relying on all that I Am. Endure to the end in obedience, and you will fulfill My will.
I have already won the victory for you. I will make you strong and victorious over every weakness, for the triumph will be great and will glorify the Father. Let Me give you eyes to see Me standing with you.

May 24

Altar of Remembrance

I will remember the works of the Lord; Surely I will remember
Your wonders of old.
I will also meditate on all Your work, And talk of Your deeds.
—*Psalm 77:11-12 (NKJV)*

See also: Psalm 103:2   Psalm 105:5

I Am the God of Abraham, Isaac, and Jacob who blesses you. See how much I have blessed you, and do not forget all My benefits. Look and see My hand upon your life.
Build Me an altar and worship Me for all that I have done. Worship Me, for I Am the God who is faithful to fulfill every promise I have spoken. As you meet Me at the altar of remembrance, I will bless you with the understanding of My faithfulness.

May 25

Heavenly Blessings

The blessing of the Lord makes one rich, And He adds no sorrow with it.
—Proverbs 10:22 (NKJV)

See also: Ephesians 1:3-8   Hebrews 12:16   Revelation 12:11

You are a sojourner, blessed with My Holy Spirit. Your blessings are lasting, for they are eternal. This is your birthright—esteem it as a greater treasure than your present circumstances.

Hold fast to all that I have promised you in difficult times, and wait for My blessings. I love you and will turn every curse into a blessing. I have pledged to you My everlasting love and faithfulness.

Rule over every evil that comes against you by finding your delight in My blessings. Pray in the difficult days, but do not forget the word of your testimony—My mercy, forgiveness, and grace that have covered your life. I Am your blessing.

May 26

Ask Me for Truth

For the law was given through Moses, but grace and truth came through Jesus Christ.
—*John 1:17 (NKJV)*

See also: John 14:6   John 18:37   Romans 5:10

I have written the story of My love for all to read and believe. The way is straight, and the path is narrow. This path is open to all who believe in Me and confess that I Am the God who created the universe, and that I Am the Way.

There is only one way, for if there were another, truth would cease to be truth. I came into the world for this purpose: to reveal Truth. I came to offer the sacrifice required to reconcile the whole world to Myself. I sent My Son to pay the price of redemption. The price was great, for it was purchased with the blood of the Lamb.

I Am ever-living, for the grave could not hold My Son. He conquered death and opened the way back to all that is true.

May 27

Life Immortal

Jesus said to her, 'I am the resurrection and the life. He who believes in Me, though he may die, he shall live.'
—John 11:25 (NKJV)

See also: Romans 2:7   1 Corinthians 15:54-57   2 Timothy 1:10

Your life is eternal by My design, and immortality with Me is My gift to you. I Am alive in you, and together we will live—now and forever.

Let My Word strengthen your mortal body each day. Walk with Me in the power of My resurrection life, and the enemy will give way as we enjoy our sweet communion together.

Let your heart grasp the eternal promises I have given you. True joy is knowing that eternity is real—and it is yours.

May 28

Prepare the Way

The voice of one crying in the wilderness: 'Prepare the way of the Lord; Make straight in the desert a highway for our God.'
—*Isaiah 40:3 (NKJV)*

See also: Matthew 3:3   John 20:27   1 John 5:4

Rise up and take your place in this mighty army—ready to prepare the way for My entrance. Clear the path, for the time has come to do great exploits with your God.
Let nothing hinder you now. Put away doubt and fear. Look upon Me and see with your own eyes what I have accomplished. This is the time for My disciples to see Me as I Am—the glorified Lord of Hosts.
I will give power to those who believe, to overcome and deliver others from bondage. Gather every stone from your path and remove it, for the King of Glory is coming!

May 29

Strengthen Yourself

Now David was greatly distressed, for the people spoke of stoning him, because the soul of all the people was grieved, every man for his sons and his daughters. But David strengthened himself in the Lord his God.
—1 Samuel 30:6 (NKJV)

See also: Psalm 91:1   1 John 5:4   Acts 17:6

My thoughts that flow to you must be deeply examined and pondered, for I desire to do marvelous things with you. Let your wisdom and counsel be from Me. You who know Me will again turn the world upside down for My glory. While the earth trembles at the news concerning Israel, remember that My promises never fail. You who know the signs of the times are commanded to rejoice. I want to see My children walking with Me in awe and in the reverence of My Name. I Am the Holy One of Jacob, and you will no longer be discontent as you accept My instruction. I will pour out My Spirit on you as you make Me your stronghold and come under the shadow of My wing. You will no longer be oppressed, for you know My Word and believe it. Wait, and expect My victory, My favor, My love, and My peace. These things come to you as the result of our unbroken fellowship.

May 30

My Desire Is Jesus

> Yet indeed I also count all things loss for the excellence of the knowledge of Christ Jesus my Lord, for whom I have suffered the loss of all things, and count them as rubbish, that I may gain Christ and be found in Him, not having my own righteousness, which is from the law, but that which is through faith in Christ, the righteousness which is from God by faith; that I may know Him and the power of His resurrection, and the fellowship of His sufferings, being conformed to His death, if, by any means, I may attain to the resurrection from the dead.
> —*Philippians 3:8-11 (NKJV)*

I have put these desires into your heart:

- To know Jesus more deeply by being acquainted with Him.
- To recognize and understand Him more fully.
- To be found in Him and known as in Him.
- To have His righteousness.
- To know the power of His resurrection in your life.

May 31

The Mysteries Of Heaven

> And He said, " To you it has been given to know the
> mysteries of kingdom of God,
> But to the rest it is given in parables, that
> 'Seeing they may not see, And hearing they may not understand.'
> —*Luke 8:10 (NKJV)*

See also: Matthew 13:11   1 Corinthians 2:16

Your goal is to see Me. You will begin to see eternal things by closing your eyes to the things of this world and opening them to the things of heaven, keeping your conscience sensitive to Me. Let the mind of Christ be in you. Be still, listen, and see, for it has been granted to you to know and perceive the mysteries of heaven. Keep this in your heart and ponder it.

June 1

A Heart Sacrifice

> And it came to pass, when the sun went down and it was dark, that behold, there appeared a smoking oven and a burning torch that passed between those pieces. On the same day the Lord made a covenant with Abram, saying: 'To your descendants I have given this land, from the river of Egypt to the great river, the River Euphrates.'
> —*Genesis 15:17-18 (NKJV)*

See also: Psalm 77:6   Hebrews 8:10-11   Hebrews 13:20-21

I Am the covenant-keeping God, the One who guards your heart in truth.
You can trust Me to reveal what lies within you.
Come, and lay every piece of your heart before Me.
Wait until My truth comes and burns away every lie.
Let the wind of My Spirit blow across your heart, for I desire it to be free—kept and guarded by Me.
Today, I Am drawing you into deeper agreement with My will than ever before.
Trust Me to keep your heart in all that I Am.

June 2

In Love

> I in them, and You in Me; that they may be made perfect in one, and that the world may know that You have sent Me, and have loved them as You have loved Me.
> —*John 17:23 (NKJV)*

See also: 1 Corinthians 13:13   1 John 4:12-18

Love is a matter of the heart, not the mind.
Ask Me for the grace to love Me back with a perfect love—a love wholly consecrated to Me.
My love must be perfected in you for My peace to reign, for peace is the fruit of a heart made right, united with Me in love.
Perfect love is your heart returning to Mine, again and again, in every way.
It is complete reliance upon My love—so secure, so whole, that it cannot help but be returned.

June 3

Alliance

Behold, I give you the authority to trample on serpents and scorpions, and over all the power of the enemy, and nothing shall by any means hurt you.
—*Luke 10:19 (NKJV)*

See also: Matthew 12:26-30

In questioning My strength, you give credence to your enemy. I Am not in any agreement where you have given Satan consideration. I Am calling you to stand and fight against the powers of evil, but you cannot do it without authority. I Am the power and authority in your life. Come over to My side and be My ally. The enemy only holds the influence you allow. Turn your heart fully toward Me and let nothing divide your trust. Say "Amen" and agree with Me. I have called you to fight and be courageous.

Keep your eyes fixed on Me, not on your enemy.

Fight in My strength and for My glory, for you will be victorious in your alliance with Me.

June 4

Chains of Obligation

> And in the process of time it came to pass that Cain brought an offering of the fruit of the ground to the Lord. Abel also brought of the firstborn of his flock and of their fat. And the Lord respected Abel and his offering, but He did not respect Cain and his offering. And Cain was very angry, and his countenance fell.
> —*Genesis 4:3-5 (NKJV)*

See also: Psalm 84:2-3   John 4:24

I have never obligated you, nor commanded you to come to Me out of duty. It is not discipline that I seek, but your heart. It is your heart that should urge you to come—a yearning for My companionship, a longing to find the satisfaction that cannot be found in any other way.

Be honest. You have not done enough to come to Me, for I have never required it as a ritual or performance. Offerings made without the heart are like the offering of Cain—without regard before Me. All that I ask is your heart in worship, for true worship is in Spirit and in Truth.

You may come to Me out of need, not out of obligation. I Am your satisfaction, your help, and your joy—approach Me this way. When you sense My compelling, come. When you feel the yearning, come. When you hear Me calling, *"Come away, My beloved."*

June 5

Overflow

He who did not spare His own Son, but delivered Him up for us all, how shall He not with Him also freely give us all things?
—Romans 8:32 (NKJV)

See also: Psalm 16:11   John 7:38-39

I see your heart as a cup that overflows.
Give freely, and keep on giving, and I will continue to pour in more.
I work through the overflow of My life within you.
When you are in need, come and rest beside the still waters I provide.
I Am deeply concerned with your fullness.
I want your heart to burst forth like a river of living water that cannot be restrained.
Never doubt the joy I have placed within you.
You are meant to live a life that overflows.

June 6

Above All

Restore to me the joy of Your salvation, And uphold me by Your generous Spirit.
—*Psalm 51:12 (NKJV)*

See also: John 15:4   Ephesians 1:3-14

Let your love for Me draw you into greater faith.
I will give the increase—only believe.
You will be blessed, and I will restore your joy; indeed, you will become My joy.
Rise above the things of the earth and abide in Me.
To you, the one I love so dearly, heaven itself awaits.

June 7

Faith

Now if God so clothes the grass of the field, which today is, and tomorrow is thrown into the oven, *will He* not much more *clothe* you, O you of little faith?
—*Matthew 6:30 (NKJV)*

See also: Psalm 107:25-30   Hebrews 10:38-39

Even though faith looks to the unseen, it is not, as you have supposed, merely to claim a better outcome or to escape your circumstances. Faith awakens an awareness of My nearness that enables you to trust Me more deeply. You cannot have faith without fully trusting Me.

Allow Me access to every part of your life. Look carefully—have you withheld from Me any area where you feel weak? Trust Me, and you will continue with Me, even in your weakness, to the higher ground of greater faith. I Am here to take your hand and help you walk upon the high and narrow places without fear of falling.

The more you release fear and doubt by trusting in My love for you, the more faith will be given to you. I keep you through every storm, strengthening you as you cry out to Me. You cannot have more faith unless you are willing to go with Me into unsafe places.

I love it when you come to the end of your own efforts and run to My feet, calling My Name—so I can lift you up, dry your tears, and draw you near. Love is the heart of faith. Say that you love Me more than you fear any trial.

June 8

Clothed in Dignity

To console those who mourn in Zion,
To give them beauty for ashes,
The oil of joy for mourning,
The garment of praise for the spirit of heaviness,
That they may be called trees of righteousness,
The planting of the Lord, that He may be glorified.
— *Isaiah 61:3 (NKJV)*

See also: Isaiah 61:10   Revelation 3:18

You cannot see your own nakedness without the help of another. When confronted, do not cover yourself with feigned modesty. The opinions of others cannot help you, for they see and judge only by outward appearance. If you want to be clothed in beauty—modestly fit for My scrutiny—accept My opinion. I have shown you how to walk with Me: in humility, love, and mercy. I alone clothe you in robes of white, making you right before Me. I give you beauty so that you will not be found naked, but clothed in dignity. Walk carefully before Me, seeking only My approval. Listen to the counsel of others with an open heart, but ask Me again what I think. Know the condition of your own heart. I Am the One who corrects My children, and I Am the One who covers every flaw with mercy and grace.

June 9

My Promised Bride

For I am persuaded that neither death nor life, nor angels nor principalities nor powers, nor things present nor things to come, nor height nor depth, nor any other created thing, shall be able to separate us from the love of God which is in Christ Jesus our Lord.
—*Romans 8:38-39 (NKJV)*

See also: Ephesians 3:17-19   Revelation 21:2-9

I Am the God of Love who says, *I love you far more than you can know right now.* Trust Me and believe Me for all that is still unseen. I will reveal My love to you as you search for My heart and open your own to Me.
There are many who cannot yet say they love Me as you do, for their expectations of Me are small. Their knowing of Me is limited by distrust of their own hearts, and many walk in unbelief. I long to restore these back to Me in love. So I Am telling all My loved ones to come to Me—with great expectancy and with a longing for more of their God. Say with Me, *"All that I have allowed is for your good."* I Am asking you to be My Bride. **Marry Me.**

June 10

Wedding Chamber

For as a young man marries a virgin, So shall your sons marry you; And as the bridegroom rejoices over the bride, So shall your God rejoice over you.
—*Isaiah 62:5 (NKJV)*

See also: Song of Songs 4:5   Matthew 25:10   2 Thessalonians 3:3

You are My chosen one, and I have given you the key to the entrance of the wedding chamber, where I pour out My love upon you. This is the place of love I have prepared for you, so come in and meet Me here, in this secret chamber lit with the flame of our love.

As you go to find the door, tell others of your great joy! Tell them, *"I have been found and chosen by True Love. A great Love is mine, and He has promised me His faithfulness. I have been rescued from despair and emptiness. I am filled with His promised love that will never be unfaithful or disloyal."*

Unlock the door and turn on the celebration lights of expectancy. Wait for Me, for the season of anticipation has begun. I Am coming soon! In joyful preparation, decorate our abode with lights of hope and set the table, for our communion is to be often.

Do not let an intruder enter through the back door. I Am your True Love, and I will not fail you or be unfaithful. Be secure, My beloved, knowing that you are My Bride in waiting.

June 11

Unfailing Faith

Then the whole congregation of the children of Israel complained against Moses and Aaron in the wilderness.
—Exodus 16:2 (NKJV)

See also: Exodus 34:6   Numbers 32:9   Proverbs 16:20   Luke 22:31-32

I allow circumstances that will try your faith to reveal who I Am in your life. Do not be confused by what I allow, or call evil good and good evil, for I Am Good. Believe in My goodness over your life and trust Me.

Do not wander through this wilderness complaining about your circumstances when I Am giving you the choice to hold onto what is good and trust Me. Look not to the fear of the unknown, but to all that I have promised you. Remember what I have already done for you and take courage, knowing that I fight for you.

My plan is to make you victorious, for I must have overcomers. Believe Me. Stand against Satan in perseverance. I will not fail you.

June 12

At My Table

> And as they were eating, Jesus took bread, blessed and broke it, and gave it to the disciples and said, 'Take, eat; this is My body.' Then He took the cup, and gave thanks, and gave it to them, saying, 'Drink from it, all of you. For this is My blood of the new covenant, which is shed for many for the remission of sins.'
> —*Matthew 26:26-28 (NKJV)*

See also: John 6:51   Mark 14:33   Philippians 3:10

I Am here. Ask Me to be your guest as you come to My table. See Me sitting across from you to fellowship with you. Come, take the bread in your hand and let Me place it upon your lips. Eat, for you are one with Me. I Am the Bread of Heaven that sustains your life.

Now take the cup. You have tasted suffering and shared in My sorrow, but know that this cup is also our joy. This cup of suffering carried Me through My darkest hour, for I saw the joy of knowing you. Our relationship is worthy of this cup. Never forget—sorrow may last for the night, but joy comes as surely as the dawn, bringing with it the light of rejoicing.

Come, My love. Let My hands surround your face as you drink deeply of this cup. Now we are one. Let My life sustain yours as we fellowship together. Invite Me back tomorrow.

June 13

All Things

> Cast your burden on the LORD,
> And He shall sustain you;
> He shall never permit the righteous to be moved.
> —*Psalm 55:22 (NKJV)*

See also: John 14:17   John 16:13   1 Corinthians 2:16

All things are Mine to give to those who believe. I have done great things for you so that you would learn that I Am your burden bearer. I have proven Myself as your Savior so that you no longer need to struggle.

Do not believe the lies of the enemy. Trust only in My truth. You must learn to discern truth in every area of your thought life. Give Me Lordship, and I will give you the ability to hear truth.

I Am with you and fighting for you. Stand with Me.

June 14

My Children

At that time the disciples came to Jesus, saying, 'Who then is greatest in the kingdom of heaven?' Then Jesus called a little child to Him, set him in the midst of them, and said, 'Assuredly, I say to you, unless you are converted and become as little children, you will by no means enter the kingdom of heaven. Therefore whoever humbles himself as this little child is the greatest in the kingdom of heaven.'
—*Matthew 18:1-4 (NKJV)*

See also: Romans 8:14   Ephesians 5:8   Hebrews 2:13

You were made for My pleasure; let Me be the delight of your soul. You are accepted, so come to Me eagerly without pretense or concerns of your own making. I Am your Abba, so be willing to ask and hear from Me, and you will truly come to know Me as I Am.

I Am longing for your childlike trust and love. This is the foundation of My Kingdom. See yourself as I created you to be—a child born out of My own nature, before Me in love, a child of light.

I tell you now, the Bridegroom will soon say, "Here I Am with the children You have given Me." You will be among them as My crowning glory.

June 15

Prepare, My Bride

And take the helmet of salvation, and the sword of the Spirit, which is the word of God.
—*Ephesians 6:17 (NKJV)*

See also: Hebrews 4:12

My Bride, you possess a magnificent sword. Take it and cut through the darkness. The power of this Sword is every word that proceeds from My mouth. Take up this mighty weapon and stand. Stand armed with the Sword of Truth.
Do not hesitate to wield it, for hesitation dulls its edge. Speak what I have spoken, and light will pierce the shadows. Every word you release in faith carries the weight of My authority and the sound of victory.

June 16

Eyes of Love

**Arise, shine; for your light has come!
And the glory of the Lord is risen upon you.**
—*Isaiah 60:1 (NKJV)*

See also: Song of Songs 1:15   2 Corinthians 1:2   Colossians 1:3

I see you as transferred into My Kingdom of Light. There is no darkness here. Walk in My light, and others will see Me. I see you as My Father's love gift, a treasure given into My hands.
I see you, My Bride, and I have betrothed you to Myself in great jealousy. I see you as My child, wearing the crown that I have placed upon your head. See yourself sitting beside Me through the eyes of My love.

June 17

God's Peace

You will keep him in perfect peace, Whose mind is stayed on You, Because he trusts in You.
—*Isaiah 26:3 (NKJV)*

See also: John 14:27   Philippians 4:7   Colossians 3:15

It is My peace that your body craves and your spirit longs for. My perfect peace is yours for the asking. This peace surpasses all understanding because it is greater than every circumstance.

The world and your enemy seek to rob you of peace, for without it, hearts grow weary and minds lose hope. Many of My children are sick and despairing because they have not learned to abide in My Presence where true peace resides.

Do not be conformed to this world, but come out of its chaos and turmoil. Stay in My peace—the place you have already known. My peace makes your spirit whole, your mind steady, and your body strong. It is the antidote to every sickness and trouble of this world.

June 18

My Image

> This is the book of the genealogy of Adam. In the day that God created man, He made him in the likeness of God. He created them male and female, and blessed them and called them Mankind in the day they were created.
> —*Genesis 5:1-2 (NKJV)*

See also: 2 Corinthians 5:17   Colossians 3:10-11

I have designed you; you are My creation, beautiful to behold. I look at who you are—and who you will be—eternally. Your vision of yourself has been marred by the lies of the enemy and the weight of earthly experience.

You are My new creation, made to bear My image through transformation. Like the butterfly, you are changed in the secret place, where My love surrounds you and you are cocooned in My presence. The invisible work of My hands is bringing forth the visible beauty of who you truly are.

As your life becomes hidden in Mine, transformation continues. What is unseen now will soon be revealed as glory. You are My beautiful, free creation. Behold the wonder of what you are becoming as you dwell with Me.

June 19

Light and Life

Your word is a lamp to my feet And a light to my path.
—Psalm 119:105 (NKJV)

See also: Matthew 25:1-8   Luke 12:35-36   John 8:12

The oil of My Spirit burns continuously, driving away every shadow along your path. The oil in the lampstand is the sevenfold Spirit of Wisdom. Take the oil I give for your own lamp, and light it with passion for Me and My Word.

My Word will illuminate your path as you walk, holding the lamp fueled by My Spirit. This light keeps you ready for My soon return. When you see another whose lamp burns dimly, encourage them to seek more of the oil that I freely give. I Am still the Light of the world, and those who walk with Me will never walk in darkness.

June 20

Five Gates

He makes me to lie down in green pastures; He leads me beside the still waters.
—*Psalm 23:2 (NKJV)*

See also: Matthew 7:13-14   John 10:7-9   Acts 3:2-7

At the Gate Beautiful, My power to heal is made known.
At the Sheepfold Gate, you enter into My rest. Here, I meet every need of your time and give you space to rest with Me.
At the Narrow Gate, you enter into My approval, and I anoint you.
At the Gate of Thanksgiving, you enter into My praise.
At the Heavenly Gate, My glory is revealed as we sit together.
I paid the entrance price for these gates with great cost so that you might know My love.

June 21

Seeing the Good

And one of them, when he saw that he was healed, returned, and with a loud voice glorified God,
—*Luke 17:15 (NKJV)*

See also: Psalm 33:8   Psalm 103:8   Luke 8:41   Colossians 3:15

There is no need for you to fight or struggle—just be in awe of Me. I Am mercy and grace, abounding in forgiveness and goodness. Look away from your circumstances, come running, and fall at My feet.

When you see Me rightly, the enemy will fear you. Satan will no longer convince you that evil will prevail, for you will be convinced of My goodness that never changes nor fails. Remember all that I have done for you and be thankful. Be the one who returns and worships Me.

Faith arises in the atmosphere of worship and gratitude. Seeing the good dispels the darkness.

June 22

Joy That Overtakes

When anxiety was great within me, Your consolation brought me joy.
—*Psalm 94:19 (NKJV)*

See also: Psalm 23:5   Psalm 28:7   Psalm 34:8

My joy fuses My heart to yours, overriding every difficult circumstance and turning hardship into praise. You have My promise that joy will overtake you, bringing times of refreshing to your soul.

I restore what was lost and even what was destroyed, giving you gladness and jubilation in place of tragedy. Let joy overtake you as I delight in revealing My faithfulness to you.

I long to fill your empty cup to overflowing with joy as you learn to drink deeply of My goodness. Taste and see that I Am good—come and enjoy Me.

June 23

More

I have come that they may have life, and that they may have it more abundantly.
—John 10:10 (NKJV)

See also: Philippians 3:12-15   Isaiah 61:3   Psalm 45:7

I Am moving. You need to know the ways in which I have moved—both now and in the past. I Am moving in your life and in the world around you. I will reveal more of Myself as you learn how, where, and why I move. Move forward into your destiny with Me.

I Am your oil supply. The oil of My Spirit gives you more joy and freedom—an overflow that touches others. Opportunities open through the anointing of My oil.

I Am the rest that restores you. Rest from striving and receive more—more healing, more joy, more of Me. Relax, release, and relent in My presence.

June 24

The Crown

Finally, there is laid up for me the crown of righteousness, which the Lord, the righteous Judge, will give to me on that Day, and not to me only but also to all who have loved His appearing.
—2 Timothy 4:8 (NKJV)

See also: James 1:12   Revelation 3:10-12

Many have received the crown of righteousness without realizing it is the victor's crown.
They have not yet known its power or its joy.
This is the crown I give to all who wait—the crown of My acceptance for patient endurance.
I give it to those who have stood the test.
Let nothing hinder you from receiving what I have prepared.

June 25

Heaven's Glory

Now after six days Jesus took Peter, James, and John, and led them up on a high mountain apart by themselves; and He was transfigured before them.
—Mark 9:2 (NKJV)

See also: Matthew 17:1-8   John 17:16

I Am all that is glorious.
Set your thoughts on the heavenlies and ponder the things above.
You will become My ambassador as you grow familiar with our eternal abode.
Let your mind rise to where I Am.
Walk upon higher ground and behold the beauty of the everlasting.
I long to reveal more to you as you turn away from darkness and gaze into heaven's light.
Come, sit with Me, and I will reveal Myself to you as I did to Peter, James, and John.
I will show you My glory as you delight yourself in My presence.

June 26

The Pearls

Who, when he had found one pearl of great price, went and sold all that he had and bought it.
—Matthew 13:46 (NKJV)

See also: 1 Peter 4:12-14

Everything of great value is tested and tried.
The jewels of life are formed by those who choose to overcome, not merely survive.
Those I love, I beautify through the tests that bring them into greater splendor.
Like the pearl, their worth is produced through time and endurance.
The irritants of this life—when surrounded by My protection—become the very substance of their beauty.
The knowledge of My goodness keeps them from despair.
They are known both here and in heaven for their true value.
How beautiful are My pearls!

June 27

In Waiting

Wait on the Lord; Be of good courage, And He shall strengthen your heart; Wait, I say, on the Lord!
—*Psalm 27:14 (NKJV)*

See also: Psalm 37:4-5   Psalm 62:5-8   Proverbs 16:9

Your one need is to anticipate My going with you, so that you do not move ahead of Me.
It is My joy for you to know Me as the ever-present God that I Am.
I Am what will come to pass, what will take place, what will be, and what will exist.
Do not look back at your past, for there is no life for you there, and I Am not found in it.
Your future holds only the hope of what I will yet do.
Therefore, wait in expectancy, trusting in the authority of who I Am.
You do not know the way except by Me, for I Am the Way, the Truth, and the Life you seek.
I Am your very life.
Each moment you set your heart to seek Me as such, you will find joy in the way ahead.
Open your heart and mind to realize that I Am in every detail of your day.
Walk with Me—laying all at My feet: your plans, your dreams, your hopes—and watch as I make them Mine.

June 28

Protection

Order the buckler and shield, And draw near to battle!
—*Jeremiah 46:3 (NKJV)*

See also: Ephesians 6:11-17   Hebrews 4:12

Your mind is the battleground of victory or defeat.
Let Me keep you in perfect peace, and the evil one will not torment your thoughts.
Your heart is the target—vulnerable to the darts and arrows of the enemy.
So put on the breastplate of righteousness.
Your heart has been wounded for lack of knowing Me as your righteousness, but let My approval heal and restore it.
The very core of your being was made for truth.
Fasten the belt of truth around you, for it is given to protect and steady your soul.
Do not let the evil one deceive you.
Ask Me, for I Am Truth.
Come, let us reason together.
What I reveal to you will set you free from the lies you have believed.
Then lift up the shield of faith—faith that believes My words and acts upon them.
Take up the sword of the Spirit, My spoken Word to you, for these words carry the power to perform My will in your life.

June 29

A Heavenly Perspective

Even when we were dead in trespasses, He made us alive together with Christ, and raised us up together, and made us sit together in the heavenly places in Christ Jesus.
—*Ephesians 2:5-6 (NKJV)*

See also: Ephesians 1:3   Ephesians 1:20   Ephesians 3:10

I Am making Myself manifest to those who enter My realm—who no longer count the things of earth as their only reality, but rise above to where I Am. One with Me, they step into the wonderful possibility, delight, and joy of heaven.

I will make My Name known—yes, even famous in these last days—through the miraculous.

Your days will be filled with wonder, for you are a child of faith, chosen to see from heaven's perspective.

June 30

Seeking Wisdom

> Wisdom is the principal thing; Therefore get wisdom. And in all your getting, get understanding. Exalt her, and she will promote you; She will bring you honor, when you embrace her. She will place on your head an ornament of grace; A crown of glory she will deliver to you.
> —*Proverbs 4:7-9 (NKJV)*

See also: Proverbs 8:1-19   2 Peter 1:3

I Am the voice that calls to you at every crossroad, giving you the understanding you need to take the higher road.
I Am Wisdom—the gate that opens heaven's door as you let go of your own ways to enter into Mine.
Seek understanding rather than more knowledge.
Remind your soul to pursue wisdom, for I desire to be your Teacher.
I will keep you from error by giving you the right words to speak at the right time.
I alone will guard you from false humility and pride.
All My children listen to My wisdom as earthly children listen to their fathers.

All That I Am

July 1

The Exchange

Come, and let us return to the Lord; For He has torn, but He will heal us; He has stricken, but He will bind us up.
After two days He will revive us; On the third day He will raise us up, That we may live in His sight.
Let us know, Let us pursue the knowledge of the Lord. His going forth is established as the morning; He will come to us like the rain, Like the latter and former rain to the earth.
—*Hosea 6:1-3 (NKJV)*

See also: John 11:25   Hebrews 4:12

I Am the One who will exchange your pierced heart for a new and better one—My own. When you die to yourself, you will truly live in Me. Allow Me to pierce your heart with truth, and from that wound will flow your freedom—a well of life-giving water. Whenever you are wounded, come to Me and let Me bind your heart with My healing. When you feel as though you might die from what I have allowed, remember that I Am the Resurrection and the Life. Many deny their pain and their need for a Physician, yet I long for you to come to Me as My child, knowing your greatest need is always My touch. I Am exchanging My hurts, My wounds, even My scars for your wholeness.

July 2

As I Am

And I will give you the keys of the kingdom of heaven, and whatever you bind on earth will be bound in heaven, and whatever you loose on earth will be loosed in heaven.
—*Matthew 16:19 (NKJV)*

See also: John 17:11   1 Peter 2:9   Psalm 8:5   Song of Songs 6:3

I have freed you from guilt and condemnation so that you may rise up and declare, "I am my Beloved's, and He is mine!" You are loved and called to be as I Am in this world—to reign with Me. I have given you the keys of My Kingdom to unlock doors and set you free. Rise up in newness of life and reflect My nature. We are one, not two. I Am glorious. I Am light. You are My reflection, for I have placed My glory within you. Stand in this knowledge, and as you do, I will make you more like Me.

July 3

My Child

> But Jesus called them to *Him* and said, "Let the little children come to Me, and do not forbid them; for of such is the kingdom of God."
> —*Luke 18:16 (NKJV)*

See also: Luke 9:46-48   John 1:12   2 Corinthians 4:6

I made you My child, for I have no adult children. I created you to be childlike, for the many gifts I've given you could easily intimidate others. I Am asking you to drop the walls that hide your true identity. Become My child again—trusting, open, and unguarded. I Am your protection; I know you, and I keep you. Lay down your defenses, for I long to see you free. I have much for you to do and to say. You are a child of the day, and I Am your Father of Lights. Walk before Me with eyes that look for the good in yourself and in others. Only then can you live true to who you are. You are a part of Me, created in My image to shine in the darkness.

July 4

Understanding

All things have been delivered to Me by My Father, and no one knows the Son except the Father. Nor does anyone know the Father except the Son, and the one to whom the Son wills to reveal Him.
—*Matthew 11:27 (NKJV)*

See also: John 16:13   1 Corinthians 2:7-16

It is by My Spirit that I reveal hidden things to your spirit. I make known what is Mine and transmit it to you, for you are greatly loved in the Son. It is through My Spirit—who searches and explores all that belongs to Me, even the deepest depths of My counsel—that revelation flows. Learn to be taught by My Spirit, for I Am the Spirit of Truth and Revelation.

July 5

Good Fruit

He shall be like a tree Planted by the rivers of water, That brings forth its fruit in its season, Whose leaf also shall not wither; And whatever he does shall prosper.
—*Psalm 1:3 (NKJV)*

See also: Proverbs 11:30

You are a tree of My own planting. I have placed you beside still waters, where you are nourished by the living water of My Word. Your roots will grow deep into the soil of My wisdom. From our time together, good fruit will come—if you are patient with yourself and listen carefully to Me. Allow Me to tend and prune away anything that spoils our relationship, for I Am looking for fruit in this season of your life. Judge rightly, and look only for fruit in your life and in the lives of others. Every good tree that bears fruit is My work and My planting. Every good tree is known by its fruit.

July 6

Chosen

For you are a holy people to the Lord your God, and the Lord has chosen you to be a people for Himself, a special treasure above all the peoples who are on the face of the earth.
—*Deuteronomy 14:2 (NKJV)*

See also: Matthew 24:46   James 2:5   Revelation 17:14

You will clear the way for others to come closer to Me and climb higher with Me. It is now time to remove the limits of your own thinking and look beyond your horizons. Look with Me and see what I have placed into your hands. I Am calling you to a great journey, born from your heart's desire for a crown to lay at My feet. Do not let your own mind hinder you. Keep your focus on Me, and you will stand in awe of all that I will do with and through you. I Am laying before you great opportunities to believe Me. It is time to work, to play, and to be about your Father's business with great joy and holy passion.

July 7

Feelings

You shall love the Lord your God with all your heart, with all your soul, and with all your strength.
—Deuteronomy 6:5 (NKJV)

See also: Song of Songs 8:6-7   John 17:13   Ephesians 3:18-19

I Am your portion and your joy in this life. My joy will fill your heart so that you may be one with Me. I long for My children to know Me in this reality—for I Am found in your experience of Me. Make your pursuit of Me your greatest passion. Let your love rise and return to Me; never let it grow cold, but let it burn ever brighter. My love is a consuming fire. I Am a passionate God, and you were born out of a passion that cannot be quenched. Return My love, for I burn with love for you.

July 8

Good God

Then He said, 'I will make all My goodness pass before you, and I will proclaim the name of the Lord before you. I will be gracious to whom I will be gracious, and I will have compassion on whom I will have compassion.'
—*Exodus 33:19 (NKJV)*

See also: Psalm 31:19   Matthew 7:7-11

I Am the source of every good thing.
In My goodness, you have been redeemed.
Ask of Me, believing for all that you need—and more besides.
Know Me as I truly Am, your good Father.
Keep on asking, seeking, and knocking, for in every way and at all times, I Am good.

July 9

Star Struck

Those who are wise shall shine like the brightness of the firmament, and those who turn many to righteousness like the stars forever and ever.
—Daniel 12:3 (NKJV)

See also: Philippians 2:15   1 Thessalonians 5:5   2 Peter 1:19

Like the stars in the galaxy, you are surrounded by My vast love. My loving-kindness, My thoughts, and My purposes for your life are vast in beauty. You must see yourself as My star—shining brightly and reflecting My glory. You are a light in the darkness, revealing the brilliance of My love.

I know every star by name. I placed each one in its position and in its appointed time. So it is with your life. You are Mine, and I know exactly where you are in time and space. I have placed you with purpose, for your life is significant to Me.

One star may seem small among many, yet its beauty and placement help rule the heavens. Be aware of your purpose and your placement in the time you live in. You are here for such a time as this—to bring forth light in the darkness.

July 10

Follow Me

Your ears shall hear a word behind you, saying, 'This is the way, walk in it,' whenever you turn to the right hand or whenever you turn to the left.
—*Isaiah 30:21 (NKJV)*

See also: Matthew 16:24   John 10:27   John 21:22

Come, follow Me—even into the alleyway, a path known by so few. Never mind the bareness of the way, nor the fact that not many are going with us. As I said to My disciple, *"What is that to you? Follow Me."*

Look to Me and do not be concerned with the opinions of others. Do not let their disapproval influence you in any way that I have asked you to walk with Me. Come along, to do My bidding.

When I ask you to stop, stop. When I stand before you and invite you to dance with Me, do not refuse Me. Disregard everything and cast off the bonds of your own mind that would prohibit your obedience at any moment.

July 11
Beloved of God

And when she rose up to glean, Boaz commanded his young men, saying, "Let her glean even among the sheaves, and do not reproach her. Also let grain from the bundles fall purposely for her; leave it that she may glean, and do not rebuke her."
—*Ruth 2:15-16 (NKJV)*

See also: Matthew 9:37-38   Matthew 20:12-15

I Am calling you to the harvest field—not in the heat of the day, but to glean what others have already given their all for. It is the gleaning of Ruth's work that I Am giving to you.
"Glean what I have laid down for you. I have commanded handfuls on purpose to be left in every corner of the fields. Go and take what is yours. I have made your work easy and your burden light in this last hour."
Take back what is Mine. Go, and I will give to you more than you could have imagined. It is My strength in you, My power in your words, and My Spirit upon you. Go into the field and take part in all that I Am doing.

July 12

Angels Over Us

Then he dreamed, and behold, a ladder was set up on the earth, and its top reached to heaven; and there the angels of God were ascending and descending on it.
—*Genesis 28:12 (NKJV)*

See also: 1 Kings 8:6-7   2 Chronicles 5:7-8   Psalm 61:4

There are angels in your home by assignment because of your asking. As angel wings once covered the Ark of the Covenant, there are angels' wings over you as I meet with you at the mercy seat. You often feel the effects of My angelic covering when you meet with Me.

Sometimes an angel stands quietly behind you, watching curiously at your response to My presence. Our relationship has drawn the attention of heaven. Take joy in our covenant relationship, knowing that it causes angels to wonder. They are fascinated by our sweet fellowship. You are a heavenly wonder to them.

Do not be amazed at the angels, but be in awe that you and I are one. All of heaven marvels at this mystery. Know that when your attention is on Me, angels are present and always will be.

July 13
My Arrow

The Spirit of the Lord spoke by me, And His word was on my tongue.
—*2 Samuel 23:2 (NKJV)*

See also: Isaiah 59:21   Zechariah 4:6

I have made you a sharp arrow in My hand. Submit all your thoughts and feelings to My control, or you will miss the mark. You, My arrow, must understand the power of what I have called you to be. Use My words—both written and those I give you in the moment—to strike the target. These words of Mine will wound and heal at the same time.

Know that this call, to be My arrow, is not a light thing. Opposition and persecution will follow, but be willing to be of no reputation. Be confident in knowing that you are My servant. Wait until I say you may speak for Me, then speak only My words and leave the outcome to My working.

I Am the bow, and My strength will be yours. The Word of My Spirit will strike the target perfectly.

July 14

Impossible

*For assuredly, I say to you,
Whoever says to this mountain,
Be removed and be cast into the sea,
And does not doubt in his heart,
But believes that those things he says will be done,
He will have whatever he says.
— Mark 11:23 (NKJV)*

See also: Matthew 19:26   Luke 1:37   Ephesians 3:20

Only with Me are all things possible. To live in Me and for Me in the natural realm is impossible—to love mercy, grace, and truth apart from Me is impossible. You are flesh on earth, and I Am above. All your striving is nothing, and all your worry is in vain.

I wait for you to come to your end and say, "God, my God, all is impossible." Then you will see My power. You will live, move, and have your being in Me. Mountains will move. Heaven will open. Miracles will happen.

I Am forever the same. I have told you, with Me, everything is possible.

July 15

This House

> And he built an altar there and called the place El Bethel, because there God appeared to him when he fled from the face of his brother.
> —*Genesis 35:7 (NKJV)*

This house has an altar where God meets us, where prayers are heard and hearts are prepared.
He sees and knows us in this house where His mercy, love, and compassion are felt, and His presence is known.
His children have been sent to this house for refuge, shelter, and care.
Come expecting to hear from Him, to be touched by Him, and to be healed.
Experience the unity of love among the brethren here as we share our fears, confess our faults, and pray for one another.
Expect great things from God in this house.

July 16

Immortal

"Most assuredly, I say to you, he who hears My word and believes in Him who sent Me has everlasting life, and shall not come into judgment, but has passed from death into life."
—*John 5:24 (NKJV)*

See also: John 11:24-25   Romans 6:4   Hebrews 2:14

Let My life give strength to your mortal body, and let My Word bring you life and healing. Live with Me in resurrection power and rejoice in this new life. Keep your mind fixed on eternal life in Me, for this is My joy—that you fear nothing, not even death, for I have conquered it for you.

You have been raised to walk in newness of life, both now and forever. Keep your thoughts on what is eternal, for only what is eternal will last. Walk with Me in the power of My resurrection life, and the enemy will give way as we enjoy sweet communion together.

July 17

Healing

> But He was wounded for our transgressions, He was
> bruised for our iniquities;
> The chastisement for our peace was upon Him,
> And by His stripes we are healed.
> —*Isaiah 53:5 (NKJV)*

See also: Romans 8:11   Hebrews 2:14   1 Peter 2:24

I destroyed sin and death and won the victory over everything that leads to death—sin, disease, and death itself. Ask of Me, believing all that I Am, for I Am the Victor. Rebuke sickness and disease in My Name, and let My Spirit bring you life—life abundant and overflowing.

I healed all who came to Me, and I heal today. I Am the same—yesterday, today, and forever the same. My Name is Healer. Believe in My Name and be made whole.

July 18

Lord of Victory

The Lord will fight for you, and you shall hold your peace.
—*Exodus 14:14 (NKJV)*

See also: 1 Samuel 17:47   Psalm 98:1   1 John 5:4

I Am the Victor, and you are to agree with Me that you are also victorious. Do not sit and say that you are weary, for I have not asked you to fight your enemy. If you keep fighting, you will end up wounded, weakened, and stopped in the midst of the battle. In your own determination to fight, you have become self-focused on your circumstances, and your one lack is seeing Me with you.

Search the Scriptures again to see how the battle is won, for the battle belongs to Me. I Am the Lord of Hosts. Arise out of your despair and let Me fight this battle. Go out in confidence, praising Me with songs of My power to conquer. Learn to rest in My finished work. Let the banner over you be the white flag of peaceful surrender.

Be ever thankful that your salvation is full and complete. Stand again in faith and let Me be the one thing you seek after. I desire your wholeheartedness in knowing Me as your Savior. I Am on your side.

July 19

Glory, Not Strife

So I have looked for You in the sanctuary, To see Your power and Your glory.
—Psalm 63:2 (NKJV)

See also: John 14:27   Romans 16:20

Glorify Me and do not enter into striving. I would have overcomers who know that in My glory there is no striving. Do not believe the enemy who says that all is against you now. No! I say that today, and in these days, My glory will be found by those who believe Me enough to enter into My ways of rest.

My ways are the ways of peace. Let My peace bring you directly into My presence, where you will find an entrance into My glory. Let all that hinders you from finding this entrance fall away. Find Me by entering into rest, by giving up strife and striving.

These are your glory days.

July 20

Prepare the Way

For You have armed me with strength for the battle; You have subdued under me those who rose against me.
—2 Samuel 22:40 (NKJV)

See also: 1 Chronicles 16:11   Isaiah 40:3   John 20:27

Put on what I have provided you with—strength and the honor of My Name. Rise up and take your place as a mighty army, ready to make a way that is prepared for My entrance. Clear the path, for the time has come to do great exploits for and with your God. Let nothing hinder you now, and put away doubt and fear.
As I told Thomas, "Reach out your hand and touch My wounds." Look upon Me and see with your own eyes what I have accomplished. Come and handle the Word of Life. My disciples see Me as I Am—your glorified Lord of Hosts. I stand before you now and say, "Look upon Me. See the price that I have paid." Gather up every stone in your path and take it away, for the King of Glory is coming!

July 21

A Love Song

> I will betroth you to Me forever,
> Yes, I will betroth you to Me
> In righteousness and justice,
> In lovingkindness and mercy,
> I will betroth you to Me in faithfulness,
> And you shall know the LORD.
> —Hosea 2:19-20 (NKJV)

See also: Luke 7:47

I have set My love upon you, and My love will pursue you. Know that in your darkest hour I will come to you, and I will be there for you. I Am a jealous God, and I see you as My beautiful and perfect one, whom I have chosen. Come to Me at any time.

"How?" you ask. "Through worship." This path back to My heart has been prepared for you to come into My presence. Sing, and I will fill your mouth with words of praise. Listen, and I will give you My very thoughts, to write a song that you will sing to Me as a passionate reply of love awakened out of its sleep.

You were created for this. I will win your love, and you will love Me more than many others. The day of our wedding is near, for My love for you is deeper than you can know.

July 22

Your Father

He shall cry to Me, 'You are my Father, My God, and the rock of my salvation.'
—*Psalm 89:26 (NKJV)*

See also: Isaiah 64:8   1 Corinthians 8:6   2 Corinthians 6:18

I was there even when you did not know Me as Father. My eye was on you as a child of destiny—My child. I knew you beforehand. You were Mine from your conception; therefore, I Am your Father.

My care for you is constant, and My correction is sure. My ways are for your progress so that you might know Me fully as Father God.

I Am pleased with you, My child. I love you with a constant and unfailing love. You are on My mind and in My heart. I think of you more often than you think of yourself.

July 23

Royalty

Therefore you are no longer a slave but a son, and if a son, then an heir of God through Christ.
—*Galatians 4:7 (NKJV)*

See also: 1 Peter 2:9   2 Timothy 2:12   Revelation 5:10

You are a celebrity in My Kingdom, and I expect you to know that you are the light that shines into the darkness of this world. You are becoming My star by allowing My Word to parent you and by letting Me rule over you.

Let Me feed you daily, for I have prepared for you what I know you need—and also what will delight you—so that you will not become weak in body or soul. Every morning I will instruct and encourage you, for I Am a great communicator and always available.

I love that your joy is to be with Me, for this is My great joy also. You now know that you are loved and that you are important in My Kingdom. You are growing, and I can hardly wait for you to come into your destiny, for destiny is in your blood by royal birth. You are to rule and reign with Me now and forever. You are learning every day to rule well, and I Am proud of you.

July 24

Restored

For as the Father raises the dead and gives life to them, even so the Son gives life to whom He will.
—John 5:21 (NKJV)

See also: Ephesians 2:16   Galatians 6:1   Ephesians 4:4

Anything dead can and will live again in Me. I restore hopes, dreams, health, families, and My Body also—of which you are a part. I want you to take part in My restoration work by forgiving and reconciling others back to Me.

Be a part of all that I Am doing to prepare for the wedding. I Am making one Body that is ready for the day of restoration of all things. Be ready also, and do not hinder My work. Build up, and do not be part of anything that separates or divides My Body.

Obey the prompting of My Spirit, and restore in My Name everyone whom I have placed in your path.

July 25

Respond in Love

The Shulamite

> By night on my bed I sought the one I love;
> I sought him, but I did not find him.
> "I will rise now," *I said,*
> "And go about the city;
> In the streets and in the squares
> I will seek the one I love."
> I sought him, but I did not find him.
> —Song of Songs 3:1-2 (NKJV)

See also: Proverbs 8:17   Hosea 2:15   Ephesians 3:19

Call out of love, not out of your need—for I know your need, but I long for your love. I have loved you with an everlasting love, with faithfulness that never fails. I have answered you in so many ways, and now I ask for your response.

Will you look to Me for love? Will you give to Me your devotion? This is where our love begins and ends—in your response. Become My true love and give Me your heart's devotion, and you will not be disappointed.

Like the Shulamite girl, search for Me until you find Me and hold onto Me in love, not service. Come, My Bride. The time for love is here. Respond to My love, for it is real and tangible.

July 26

My Words

> But He answered and said, "It is written, 'Man shall not live by bread alone, but by every word that proceeds from the mouth of God.'"
> —Matthew 4:4 (NKJV)

See also: John 4:10   John 6:35   John 10:166

I do not speak to you out of dead theology, for that is of the flesh. I speak to My chosen through the revelation of My words, both written and spoken. Look back in time and see that from My spoken word comes the immediate, life-giving response that changes things in this world.

My written Word is the foundation of all that I have done and all that I will do for you. My spoken Word is the fountain of living water that I promised to you. You need not study, strive, or search for the Bread of Life, for you shall partake of it. It comes down and is given to you as you live by every word that proceeds from My mouth.

Use My Word as the foundation on which you build your relationship with Me, and trust that I speak to you through every word you hear from My Spirit.

July 27

Questions

For who makes you differ from another? And what do you have that you did not receive? Now if you did indeed receive it, why do you boast as if you had not received it? You are already full! You are already rich! You have reigned as kings without us—and indeed I could wish you did reign, that we also might reign with you!
—1 Corinthians 4:7-8 (NKJV)

See also: Revelation 2:4

Contemplation:
Why are so many men of God against the moving of the Spirit—in healing, prophecy, and tongues—when these things are clearly taught in the epistles as instructions to the church for its edification?

The Response:
Men have built kingdoms of their own that they govern. They fear anything they cannot control or regulate. They are afraid of change and of criticism. They have forgotten their first love—the cry for more of Me and less of success. Their works are many and often good, but they lack the power to move beyond mere intellect. They will not risk for My Name because they are protecting their own.

July 28

A Surrendered Heart

He will sit as a refiner and a purifier of silver;
He will purify the sons of Levi,
And purge them as gold and silver,
That they may offer to the LORD
An offering in righteousness.
—*Malachi 3:3 (NKJV)*

See also: Matthew 5:8   Luke 3:16

Everything must be laid upon an altar before the fire comes down. Be willing to offer Me the things that I show you and lay them upon this altar. Surrender is the fuel for My fire upon your heart. A fire in your heart that many waters cannot quench. You will find that a surrendered heart does not have to deal with the storms of everyday life. Lay all upon the altar and I will purify your heart by My fire. A strong love will come out of your daily agreement and awareness of Me. You must have a pure heart that will beat in rhythm with Mine. Give Me your dead works and I will light a fire upon your heart that will burn with love.

July 29

Take Courage

Only be strong and very courageous, that you may observe to do according to all the law which Moses My servant commanded you; do not turn from it to the right hand or to the left, that you may prosper wherever you go.
—*Joshua 1:7 (NKJV)*

See also: Matthew 4:4   John 14:6   1 Corinthians 16:13

Keep taking time to be in My presence, for everything I Am doing is to strengthen you. I have not called you to be weak or cowardly, but to be as I Am—strong and courageous in the battle. I will give you all that you need to become victorious if you do not loosen your hold on Me.

Keep coming to Me, confessing your weaknesses, and I will be faithful to prepare the path for you to walk upon. I Am on your side, fighting for you. Keep your spiritual eyes fixed on Me.

I Am still the Way, for I Am guiding your path.

I Am still the Life, for I Am sustaining you daily.

I Am still the Truth, for in My words spoken to you, you will find your security.

July 30

Leaving

Lord, to whom shall we go, You have the words of eternal life.
—John 6:68 (NKJV)

See also: Matthew 22:31-32   John 12:26   John 17:3

Pack your bags and leave behind what is near, to reach all that is eternal. Leave behind what you call real, and become acquainted with the greater reality—valuing what is lasting over what is temporary.

The sounds of heaven are more lovely than those of the earth. The unseen is more real than what is seen. Until you pack to leave the natural, you will never arrive here.

I Am the reality your soul seeks.

I Am what endures.

Let go of knowing, and pack your bags with only the things of love.

July 31

Today

As you therefore have received Christ Jesus the Lord, so walk in Him, rooted and built up in Him and established in the faith, as you have been taught, abounding in it with thanksgiving.
—*Colossians 2:6–7 (NKJV)*

See also: Colossians 1:11   1 John 2:6

Today, I will walk on water—confident in Christ and enjoying my salvation.
Today, I will be amazed at my faith, expecting God's goodness.
Today, I will see Jesus in everything I do, and everywhere I go.
Today!
For I am rooted in His love and established in His strength, unmoved by the storms around me.
Each step I take is a testimony that Christ lives in me, and His life in me makes every day a miracle.

August 1

Ask of Heaven

But now, O Lord, You are our Father; We are the clay, and You our potter; And all we are the work of Your hand.
—*Isaiah 64:8 (NKJV)*

See also: Jeremiah 9:24   Ephesians 2:10   Hebrews 4:12

You have believed that reasoning will help you find truth, but I ask you to surrender your reasoning to Me. Your greatest need is to give Me your will, mind, and emotions. I long to be your God. Ask Me for what is higher than your own thoughts. In humility, yield all that you are, and I will rebuild all that I Am in you. You are My workmanship; I Am the potter, and you are My clay. My promise is to make you a vessel of honor for My glory. Until now you have asked so little—ask, ask of Heaven!

August 2

Be My Book

Looking unto Jesus, the author and finisher of our faith, who for the joy that was set before Him endured the cross, despising the shame, and has sat down at the right hand of the throne of God.
—*Hebrews 12:2 (NKJV)*

See also: Revelation 20:12

I Am the Author and Finisher of every life. I have written many books—those who have lived and those who now live. Some lives I have recorded by My Spirit as examples for you to follow and learn from. Study them well. There are things I Am writing, and others I Am about to write, that no one knows except My Spirit. Some life books I have published, while others remain closed and not for your scrutiny. You cannot know the deep work I Am penning upon the pages of another's life. Some of these books bear the endorsements of men, but the most significant I have endorsed for My glory. Be My book. Be open to what I will write on the next pages of your life. Take heart and let Me write something amazing in these coming chapters of your story. I will publish it for My glory.

August 3

Trampling Flowers

The voice said, "Cry out!" And he said, "What shall I cry?" "All flesh is grass, And all its loveliness is like the flower of the field. The grass withers, the flower fades, Because the breath of the Lord blows upon it; Surely the people are grass."
—Isaiah 40:6-7 (NKJV)

See also: Philippians 2:3   1 Corinthians 12:25-26   1 Peter 1:24

I have called you to walk circumspectly, to look carefully at how and where you walk, so that you do not trample My field. Some of those you barely notice are My favorite flowers. Some are bent low from lack, others are fragile from their circumstances, and some are just beginning to bud into their glory. You, My child, must take care to behold their beauty. Look around you and see these flowers of Mine as I have told you, esteeming others higher than yourself. Do not compare, condemn, or exalt yourself above another of My wonderful works.

Every soul flowering in the light of My Son is being shaped by My hand. There is a beauty you cannot yet behold—it is still forming. You do not know the heart or the soul of another, but know that I Am working. Gather the flowers around you and say, *"How beautiful are the flowers in God's field!"*

August 4

The Quest

Create in me a clean heart, O God, And renew a steadfast spirit within me. Do not cast me away from Your presence, And do not take Your Holy Spirit from me.
—*Psalm 51:10-11 (NKJV)*

See also: Matthew 6:33   Colossians 3:1   Hebrews 6:11-12

I long to bless you with a longing for Me, but you must forsake all else and make Me your greatest quest. I will bless you abundantly—beyond anything you could ever ask or imagine. As you look carefully into My Word and spend time alone with Me out of love, I will place My desires within you.

You will come to know Me as I make Myself known to you. Be determined to set Me as your one vital need, and I will fight your battles. I will cause you to stand, and you will see My deliverance.

I Am with you in this quest.

August 5

Close to You

His mouth is most sweet, Yes, he is altogether lovely. This is my beloved,
And this is my friend, O daughters of Jerusalem!
—*Song of Songs 5:16 (NKJV)*

See also: Matthew 12:50   Romans 8:29

You have invited Me into a place of intimacy—the bedroom of our home—where we share the thoughts of the day as lovers. Know that I Am ever present with you. I desire to be with you every moment, but often you shut Me out with your concerns. Yet I Am always there.

Turn and see Me, for I Am gently tapping on your shoulder. Come to Me and cast off the old thoughts that make Me seem distant. I Am your friend and your lover. We are living together in an intimate relationship. Tell Me all, and I will share My heart, My mind, and My counsel with you.

Listen to My Spirit as He woos you. My love calls to you every day—answer the call. We are best friends forever. *BFFs,* if you wish to laugh with Me.

August 6

Take My Comfort

"Comfort, yes, comfort My people!"
Says your God.
"Speak comfort to Jerusalem, and cry out to her,
That her warfare is ended,
That her iniquity is pardoned;
For she has received from the Lord's hand
Double for all her sins."
—*Isaiah 40:1-2 (NKJV)*

See also: Isaiah 61:2-3   2 Corinthians 1:3-4

Turn again and lift up another. Strengthen those who have fallen, and I will give you My very words to speak. You know Me more deeply now. Say to the downcast, *"Hope is here! Lift up your eyes and look to our God, for He is able to deliver you!"*
Comfort those who are as you once were. Take up this mantle, and I will use you as I did My servant Isaiah. My people are in need of comfort, and I have given you Mine—soft and sure, like pillows for the weary. Now, give the pillow of My comfort to those in need.

August 7

Be A Blessing

You shall not circulate a false report. Do not put your hand with the wicked to be an unrighteous witness. You shall not follow a crowd to do evil; nor shall you testify in a dispute so as to turn aside after many to pervert justice.
—*Exodus 23:1-2 (NKJV)*

See also: Matthew 18:21   Romans 12:19-20

You are Mine, and you have chosen to camp around My altar and draw near to Me. Wherever you see Balaams for hire, know that jealousy, fear, and envy are at work. Learn to discern what is good, for evil abounds in the world. Bless others, even your enemies. Never let anything but blessing be found upon your lips, and I will bless you sevenfold. You dwell under the shadow of My wing, along with others who camp around My glory. Here, you will learn to love and forgive every offense. As you do, you will bless yourself and others, for I Am the One who contributes to your welfare.

August 8

The Wedding

Then the kingdom of heaven shall be likened to ten virgins who took their lamps and went out to meet the bridegroom.
—*Matthew 25:1 (NKJV)*

See also: Matthew 25:2-13   Revelation 16:15   Revelation 19:7-8

My Bride looks into the mirror to see her image, but she is not ready. Her dress cannot be found! She wears an off-colored slip and bare feet, frantically searching for help. But I Am the One who owns the bridal suite. I will help you to be ready, My Bride, in these last moments of time.
Your maidens are arriving now to adorn you. So cease your striving. Here is your gown, your veil, and the slippers for your feet. Go forth, My Bride, in full radiance, for I have made you beautiful and complete.
Behold, I come for the one I love.

August 9

More Than Friends

You did not choose Me, but I chose you and appointed you that you should go and bear fruit, and that your fruit should remain, that whatever you ask the Father in My name He may give it to you.
—*John 15:16 (NKJV)*

See also: John 21:17

You will come to understand My love in a deeper way in this next season, My sweet child. Love will be poured out upon you—watch for it.
Because you have chosen Me (as if I needed a reason), your heart has been postured to receive more of My love. And My heart responds, *"I choose to love you right back!"*
Even as Peter once declared his love, I now invite you to go beyond friendship, for My heart desires all of your love. I Am what you need and all that you long for.
Take note of this day, for I have come to ask for your heart—we are more than friends.

August 10

These Days

Then he took the mantle of Elijah that had fallen from him, and struck the water, and said, 'Where is the Lord God of Elijah?' And when he also had struck the water, it was divided this way and that; and Elisha crossed over. Now when the sons of the prophets who were from Jericho saw him, they said, 'The spirit of Elijah rests on Elisha.' And they came to meet him, and bowed to the ground before him.
—2 Kings 2:14-15 (NKJV)

See also: 2 Kings 13:18-19   Ezekiel 11:19   Ezekiel 39:29

I will pour out My Spirit without measure upon all who believe Me—for healing, for seeing into the heavens, for provision, and for the raising of the dead in My Name. Through your testimony, even some unbelievers will see into the unseen realm.

Tap the arrows of your faith, believing Me for greater victory, for in your faith lies the measure of victory that is yours alone. These are the days of those who respond to the touch of their God.

So seek My face, fall before Me, and inquire of Me what I would have you become in My hands—in this, your day.

August 11

Gifts

As each one has received a gift, minister it to one another, as good stewards of the manifold grace of God.
—1 Peter 4:10 (NKJV)

See also: Luke 12:48   Romans 12:6-8   1 Corinthians 12:6-12

I have given you gifts that belong to the eternal realm—dreams, visions, healing, and words that flow from My Spirit. Treasure these holy things, and never allow them to become ordinary to you, for they are from above.

These gifts are not for your keeping alone; they are given to help others and to glorify Me. I have chosen you to receive the things of heaven so that, through them, you may honor Me in their use and in My using of you.

I will require an accounting of these gifts on the day you stand before Me, not to chastise you, but to reward you eternally. Keep a record of what I have given and how you have used it, so that your reward will bring glory to My Son on the day of His wedding.

Use what I have entrusted to you, and I will add more.

August 12

Fire of God

For our God is a consuming fire.
—Hebrews 12:29 (NKJV)

See also: 2 Timothy 1:6-7

I have surrounded you with people of My oil and fire. Walk, if you must, in the light of their lamps, but do not neglect the work I Am doing in your own heart and mind.

Run after Me with your whole heart. Give Me your thoughts and remain seated where I have placed you—resting in Me, safe and secure. I will not leave you for even a moment.

Rest is the litmus test of a soul in faith.

August 13

Tender Mercy

Remember, O Lord, Your tender mercies and Your lovingkindnesses, For they are from of old.
—*Psalm 25:6 (NKJV)*

See also: Psalm 40:11   John 8:4-11

You need My compassion when you are condemned by your enemies. You are often like the woman thrown at My feet by her accusers—feeling hopeless as she wept upon the ground. Then she looked and saw what I wrote in the dust. There, I inscribed words of mercy, compassion, goodness, and lovingkindness. Through these, I blot out your transgressions and silence your accusers. I Am in love with you, and I do not condemn you. As you look to Me, I look upon you and say, *"Go, and sin no more."*

Fall beneath the covering of My grace and receive the multitude of My tender mercies.

August 14

God of Wonder

In mighty signs and wonders, by the power of the Spirit of God, so that from Jerusalem and round about to Illyricum I have fully preached the gospel of Christ.
—*Romans 15:19 (NKJV)*

See also: Hebrews 2:4   Psalm 77:14   Acts 2:22

You need to marvel at our relationship, for even the angels wonder at My intervention in your life. Stand in awe of My love for you, and wonder at the grace I have poured upon your days. The God of Wonders—that is Who I Am to you.

Your need is to recognize Me as such. Do not be surprised any longer by My work in your life; instead, be thankful. Thank Me in advance, for your faith sets My work in motion. I move in wonderful ways, and what I do in your life declares Who I Am.

I Am a wondrous God. Meditate on these truths whenever doubt or despair tries to enter your heart.

August 15

My Delight

As for the saints who are on the earth, 'They are the excellent ones, in whom is all my delight.'
—*Psalm 16:3 (NKJV)*

See also: Isaiah 62:3-5   Hosea 2:19-20

I Am the Existing One who calls you *by name*. I have had compassion on you, and now I have crowned and established you. Hear Me cry out and proclaim, *"You are My delight!"*
You shall no longer think of yourself as lost or left alone. Say aloud with Me, *"His delight is in me!"* Sit with Me in the place of My favor and authority, for from there you will teach your children.
I will be to you both King and Husband, for I Am Lord and Lover.

August 16

Just Jump!

Do not fear, little flock, for it is your Father's good pleasure to give you the kingdom.
—*Luke 12:32 (NKJV)*

See also: Matthew 28:20

Every time you free-fall, I will catch you. You must abandon yourself to Me in this way to know what it feels like to be held in My arms. Each time you take such a risk, you will discover the great reward of feeling My embrace.
At times, I will even give you a gentle push so that you may leap, for I know you need help to overcome the fear of falling so far. I do this because I have great things planned for you—far higher than you have imagined. How else will I receive glory for My Name?
Your one great need is to trust Me more each day. Trusting Me for the impossible will be our shared adventure.

August 17

Call of God

And the Lord said, 'Here is a place by Me, and you shall stand on the rock. So it shall be, while My glory passes by, that I will put you in the cleft of the rock, and will cover you with My hand while I pass by.'
—*Exodus 33:21-22 (NKJV)*

See also: Psalm 62:2-7   1 Corinthians 10:4   Hebrews 5:2

Do not look to your own soul with its fleeting emotions—no, look to Me. I Am the Solid Rock of Ages. You will make spiritual progress upon all that I have revealed to you.
When you come away with Me, confess your weaknesses, but do not dwell on them. Instead, look for My grace to overcome every frail place in your heart and mind.
Dwell with Me in the heavenly places, where I will share with you the joy of My presence.

August 18

Lovely

O my dove, in the clefts of the rock, In the secret places of the cliff, Let me see your face, Let me hear your voice; For your voice is sweet, And your face is lovely.
—*Song of Songs 2:14 (NKJV)*

See also: Song of Songs 7:10

I watch everything you do in My Name. I see your heart, and I smile. You may not think I notice, but I see when you are moved by another's need.
You are My beautiful one, favored with My love. Look for Me, for I Am looking for your love. It is your love that I died for. I Am moved by your affection and hold you close to Me in these moments.
You are altogether lovely.

August 19
This Year

You have given him his heart's desire, And have not withheld the request of his lips. Selah
—*Psalm 21:2 (NKJV)*

See also: Jeremiah 31:3   1 Corinthians 2:9

This year, a new depth of My love will be revealed to you. You will feel like a teenager in love—captivated and full of wonder. Make a wish and blow in expectation, for I long to make your desires come true.

This will be a year filled with wonder and dreams fulfilled. Dance with Me into this new season with hope. Place your hand in Mine and feel My arms around your waist, holding you close.

Dream with Me again.

August 20

Steering Your Ship

*He stirs up the sea with His power,
And by His understanding He breaks up the storm.*
—*Job 26:12 (NKJV)*

See also: Psalm 107:29-31   Matthew 14:32-33

I Am your Captain at the helm, gently steering the boat of your life. Do not be anxious about where or how you are traveling. The storm is over, and now the boat moves forward, carried by the wind of My Spirit.
Look for the wind, not the destination. There is no hurry in this time with Me. I have much to share with you, and every day is important—so do not look elsewhere. I desire your fellowship and your trust.
Sail along by staying attentive to My Spirit, ignoring every other distraction. Call your spirit to align with Mine, for deep calls to deep. There will be times when the boat seems still, making no progress at all, yet that is the beauty of My presence with you in this vessel of time.
I know the course of your life, and I Am steering you toward a great harbor. Do you enjoy sailing? I know you do. So enjoy these moments with Me.

August 21

Promised Land

Every place that the sole of your foot will tread upon I have given you, as I said to Moses. From the wilderness and this Lebanon as far as the great river, the River Euphrates, all the land of the Hittites, and to the Great Sea toward the going down of the sun, shall be your territory.
—*Joshua 1:3-4 (NKJV)*

See also: 1 Samuel 17:47   2 Chronicles 20:17   Revelation 3:11

Now is the time to cross over and take new territory for the Kingdom. If you focus on the difficulties, you will never step into victory. Look instead at Who I Am and what I have done in your life.

Stop grumbling or complaining about life's hardships—I have promised you more. Take hold of what I have spoken with faith, for I will go before you and fight. Do not let fear or discouragement take root, for I have made you victorious in Me.

See what I will do as you step into battle and trust. I have placed the victor's crown upon your head.

August 22

Into the Deep

When He had stopped speaking, He said to Simon, "Launch out into the deep and let down your nets for a catch."
—*Luke 5:4 (NKJV)*

Go ahead, cast out into the deep. I Am bringing others beside you—those who will influence, inspire, and open doors for you. Some will speak truth with honesty and humility; others will cheer you on with faith and joy. Know that what I have given you is not for yourself alone, for your gifts and calling affect others. See what I Am doing, and step boldly into uncharted waters.

August 23

Cinderella

He who overcomes shall be clothed in white garments, and I will not blot out his name from the Book of Life, but I will confess his name before My Father and before His angels.
—*Revelation 3:5 (NKJV)*

See also: Psalm 139:2-12   Isaiah 60:1

Cinderella was forced to grovel in the ashes of her life. She labored under the weight of desperate circumstances, trodden down by cruelty and injustice. Yet she had been told that her Father was a man of great wealth and that she was the heiress of all He possessed. Deep within, she knew her life was not meant to be as it seemed, for everything had been stripped away by the hand of her enemy.

This cruel one delighted in her pain, making each day harder than the last. Poor Cinderella—so much unkindness and unfairness, yet she dared not complain. Then, one day, everything changed. In the garden, as she wept, her dream of attending the ball suddenly became reality.

She was clothed in beauty, her gown radiant, and she was told she was special. After one night of dancing with the Prince, she discovered her true identity. Now nothing else matters. She is no longer a victim of her circumstances. She is His Bride in waiting—His and forever royal.

August 24

In Rest

And He said, "My Presence will go *with you,* and I will give you rest."
—*Exodus 33:14 (NKJV)*

See also: Hebrews chapter 4

I Am the God who brings you into rest in every battle when you stop striving in your own strength. My power is revealed in the moments when you cease from your own effort. Let go and watch what I will do as I fight on your behalf. The soul at rest is the soul that knows victory.
Rest in Me.

August 25

Freedom Reigns

For the law of the Spirit of life in Christ Jesus has made me free from the law of sin and death.
—*Romans 8:2 (NKJV)*

See also: Galatians 5:1

You will find freedom where the flame of your love ignites your passion for all that I Am. You were created to be free—free from everything that separates you from Me.
Freedom is where your soul soars to new heights. Listen to the call of My Spirit and let freedom be your battle cry. My desire is for you to remain unchained until I return.
Let freedom reign.

August 26

The Truth or Nothing

The Spirit of truth, whom the world cannot receive, because it neither sees Him nor knows Him; but you know Him, for He dwells with you and will be in you. I will not leave you orphans; I will come to you.
—*John 14:17-18 (NKJV)*

See also: 1 Corinthians 2:16   2 Timothy 2:15

I have proven Myself to you as your Savior so that you might not struggle. Do not believe the lies of the enemy, but trust only in truth. You must learn to discern truth in every area of your thought life and let it reign over all.
Give Me Lordship, and your eyes and ears will open to truth. As you read My Word, I will reveal it to you. Let nothing but truth fill your mind.

August 27

Your Sticks

Therefore we were buried with Him through baptism into death, that just as Christ was raised from the dead by the glory of the Father, even so we also should walk in newness of life.
—*Romans 6:4 (NKJV)*

See also: Isaiah 43:19   John 15:16   1 Corinthians 3:13-15

I want you to give Me the sticks in your hands—the dead things you are still holding onto. I cannot place upon you the fire from My altar while you cling to what has no life. I desire to burn these dead things, for they carry nothing of My Spirit.

Some of these sticks are past hurts and lies, and the dryness they bring is fit only for burning. Trust Me when I say you must lay all of it upon My altar to be consumed. Then I will give you fresh things from My storehouse—new things you have not even imagined.

Let the past go, all of it. Count it only as dead wood for the fire. Lay before Me everything that hinders you from the newness of life. When I show you a stick, hand it to Me and say, *"Here is this dead thing—take it from my hand; it is Yours."*

I will trade you My thoughts for your dead reasoning, and a new future for your dead past.

August 28

Road Less Traveled

I press toward the goal for the prize of the upward call of God in Christ Jesus.
– Philippians 3:14 (NKJV)

See also: Luke 14:27

I Am your friend, so trust Me now. Do not remain distant, clinging to the ground. Your faith is on trial—shake the sand from your feet, for love trusts. Your need is to come up higher and walk the road less traveled. Those who love Me will walk the road to Calvary, fixing their eyes on Me. See My tears. I know pain and suffering; I chose it so you could know My compassion.

You cannot stay where you are. Walk on higher ground by fixing your eyes on what is to come, knowing that I Am doing a greater work within you. The things that last are unseen, revealed only as you trust Me on this narrow road. Endure the cross with Me, for resurrection life is the greatest miracle of all.

August 29

More Joy

Until now you have asked nothing in My name. Ask, and you will receive, that your joy may be full.
– *John 16:24 (NKJV)*

See also: Psalm 51:8   Isaiah 35:10   Matthew 5:6

Let My joy strengthen you, for with joy come greater conquests. Joy makes you aware of My presence and moves your heart to praise. It is My delight to see My children enter into all that I intended for them.

Trust Me today and leap forward with joyful confidence, knowing that I go before you to make your way victorious. I have heard your cry for more—but do not despise the hard things. Instead, bring Me praise and pray for greater joy to overcome every difficult situation.

With Me, your joy will be made full.

August 30

Heaven Sent

You shall walk after the Lord your God and fear Him, and keep His commandments and obey His voice; you shall serve Him and hold fast to Him.
—*Deuteronomy 13:4 (NKJV)*

See also: Matthew 24:46   Luke 11:9   Philippians 3:12

Live in communion with Me, obeying in all things and refusing agreement with the enemy. My resources are released when you allow Me to have My way.
Ask for the mind of Christ. Ask for My Spirit without limit. Do My bidding, for I Am your greatest joy this side of heaven.

August 31

Ballet Shoes & Combat Boots

> Then all this assembly shall know that the Lord does not save with sword and spear; for the battle is the Lord's, and He will give you into our hands.
> —*1 Samuel 17:47 (NKJV)*

See also: 2 Chronicles 20:17   Psalm 55:18   2 Corinthians 12:9

Are you weary? Fighting just to stay in the war will only lead to exhaustion. The battle has been long, but I stand before you now with ballet shoes in My hands, asking you to trade your combat boots of strength and pride for the beauty of these dance slippers.

It's time to give Me your boots. In these new shoes, you will dance over your troubles in My arms, following My lead in a waltz of love. These slippers will carry you effortlessly above the war zone.

Ask Me for grace, not strength, for it is My grace that will keep you going. My grace is always sufficient in your weakness. Let Me fight this battle for you, and as you become one with Me, the battle will become *our* victory.

September 1

Higher Calling

If then you were raised with Christ, seek those things which are above, where Christ is, sitting at the right hand of God. Set your mind on things above, not on things on the earth.
— *Colossians 3:1-2 (NKJV)*

Here is My invitation: come and sit beside Me in the heavenly realm where I rule. Take the place I have prepared for you. From this vantage point, you will look down and see with Me from a higher place. Remain seated here, where My mind is revealed and your soul flourishes. Higher is where you will find Me—in all My splendor.

September 2

Wait on Me

>So when the evening had come, the owner of the vineyard said to his steward, 'Call the laborers, and give them their wages, beginning with the last to the first.'
>—*Matthew 20:8 (NKJV)*
>
>See also: Matthew 20:10-16   Acts 1:8

The battle is raging in the heavens. I Am calling forth My warriors, not the faint of heart. I Am shaping you into what you were meant to be. Heaven has no room for the cowardly, the fainthearted, or the unbelieving. You will receive the same reward as those who have toiled in the heat of the day. Those who have gone before you are a great host of witnesses who have overcome. You join them through your steadfast love, and you're waiting on Me.

September 3

My Covenants

I set My rainbow in the cloud, and it shall be for the sign of the covenant between Me and the earth.
—*Genesis 9:13 (NKJV)*

See also: Genesis 12:2-3   Romans 4:16   Hebrews 13:20

See, I have set My rainbow in the sky as a sign that I keep My covenants. I blessed Abraham, and as his heir, you are blessed through faith. I will make you distinguished among the unbelieving by the blessings I place upon your life.
Take hold of your birthright and rest in My protection and provision. Be like Abraham—walking in obedient faith, knowing Me as your compensation and your great reward. My covenants of old are ever new through the everlasting blood of Jesus.

September 4

Reasons to Sing

You have put gladness in my heart, More than in the season that their grain and wine increased.
—*Psalm 4:7 (NKJV)*

See also: Psalm 33:3   Psalm 94:19   Revelation 3:11

I Am Wonderful.
I Am steering your course.
I Am the new wine of joy.
I Am the Prince of Peace.
I Am merciful.
I Am your Shield.
I Am your supply.
I Am your King.
I Am your Healer.
I Am your friend.
I Am your comfort.
I Am your courage.
I Am coming soon.

September 5

Know Me

For thus says the Lord God, the Holy One of Israel:
"In returning and rest you shall be saved;
In quietness and confidence shall be your strength."
But you would not.
—*Isaiah 30:15 (NKJV)*

See also: Psalm 16:11   Luke 10:42

I want you to know Me as your Shepherd—keeping you close enough to hear Me when I whisper. Take time to simply be with Me in quietness, and I will come and be with you. Anticipate My presence, for what I Am giving you in these moments is My very Self—let Me sustain you today.

September 6

My Heart

When I remember You on my bed, I meditate on You in the night watches.
—Psalm 63:6 (NKJV)

See also: Song of Songs 4:9   John 3:29-30   John 20:28

Today, think of Me often as you dwell in My nearness, for I have provided you a place within My heart. Remember that I Am a big God. You are My rare jewel, and your heart will grow as My presence deepens within you, for I have fashioned you for Myself that My glory may be revealed in you.
I Am the Bridegroom, and you are My bride. You need My constant love and presence realized deep within your heart. I Am not the God of another—I Am your God.

September 7

Listen to Wisdom

Let my cry come before You, O Lord; Give me understanding according to Your word.
—*Psalm 119:169 (NKJV)*

See also: Proverbs 2:2-6   Proverbs 8:6-12

I Am Wisdom—the gate that opens to heaven's door as you let go of what you think you know. Let your confidence be in Me as you seek My understanding instead of more knowledge. Remind your soul to pursue My Wisdom, for I long to be your Teacher.

I alone keep you from error by giving you insight and discernment. I keep you from making wrong judgments. I give you My thoughts as you open your heart to receive from My Spirit.

All My children listen to Wisdom.

September 8

Graduate

And when He had called His twelve disciples to Him, He gave them power over unclean spirits, to cast them out, and to heal all kinds of sickness and all kinds of disease.
—*Matthew 10:1 (NKJV)*

See also: John 14:12   Romans 15:19

Do you still see yourself as being in school? I want you to understand that you have graduated. You are no longer going out to serve Me as if it were a class assignment. What you have learned is now a way of living life with Me. You fulfill My joy as you go out in My Name, believing Me for the greater works I have promised. Those who believe will see signs and wonders in their expectation of Me.

September 9

The Sword

**Your word I have hidden in my heart,
That I might not sin against You.**
— *Psalm 119:11 (NKJV)*

See also: Ephesians 6:17   Hebrews 4:12   Revelation 2:12

I will show you how to use this sword, for it is too large, too mighty, and too beautiful for you to wield alone. You are to remain hidden behind it always, for your life is meant to be concealed and protected by Truth.

Your enemy fears this weapon, for when it is used, darkness is dispelled, oppression is lifted, and you are set free from every bondage. All fear is removed by this Sword of Truth. It is a magnificent silver blade, precious and pure.

Within this Sword lies the understanding, knowledge, and purity of My Word. In this weapon are My promises, kept and ready for your use. Stand in My strength, take up this mighty Sword, and use it as I direct you.

September 10

Say It!

A man has joy by the answer of his mouth, And a word spoken in due season, how good it is!
—*Proverbs 15:23 (NKJV)*

See also: Matthew 4:1-4   Matthew 10:27   Hebrews 4:12

I have commanded you, who know My voice, to speak My words and My will over your enemy. The enemy has no power over My spoken Word. The evil realm bows to it. The devil knows every one of My words, but the power lies in your faith to speak them—with authority, convinced of their power to save and deliver you.

Declare My Word out loud and often in the battle, knowing that at the appointed time it will defeat your adversary. My Spirit has a voice; let Him speak through you. The enemy has silenced you for too long. When you hear My Spirit's voice—just say it!

September 11

Goliath

And he shall say to them, 'Hear, O Israel: Today you are on the verge of battle with your enemies. Do not let your heart faint, do not be afraid, and do not tremble or be terrified because of them;'for the LORD your God *is* He who goes with you, to fight for you against your enemies, to save you.'
— *Deuteronomy 20:3-4 (NKJV)*

See also: Proverbs 20:5   Ephesians 6:16   Hebrews 4:12

Do you see your enemy? He has appeared to you as large as Goliath to deceive you. Tell this "Goliath" that you know the truth—that he is an imposter. Before Me you stand, and you will declare that I Am your God, who will not be mocked.
Stand with your shield of faith and say, *"My God, who has delivered me before, will be with me now."* Say to your Goliath, *"I come in the Name of the Lord of Hosts, for He fights for me."* You will prevail through faith and courage as you stand in My Name.
I Am the Lord, mighty to save. See what I will do for you when you believe Me. Your Goliath will fall by My Word in your hand, for I Am the force behind it, and it slays every giant. Trust in Me and be brave, for your giant is small—and you are meant to be My David. Run into the battle, not from it.

September 12

Marry Me

"Be silent in the presence of the Lord God;
For the day of the Lord is at hand,
For the Lord has prepared a sacrifice;
He has invited His guests."
— *Zephaniah 1:7 (NKJV)*

See also: Psalm 89:28   Isaiah 54:5

I Am coming soon for you, the one I love. Consecrate yourself to Me as the lover of your soul—the One who knows your every weakness and every victory.

Today, marry Me anew. Pledge your life to Me, vowing to be only Mine. Declare that you will not share My love with another, nor give your heart to any lesser thing.

Guard your heart and set your affections on Me. Remind yourself often that I Am yours, and you are Mine—forever.

September 13

My Grace

For by grace you have been saved through faith, and that not of yourselves; it is the gift of God.
—*Ephesians 2:8 (NKJV)*

See also: Romans 5:20-21 James 2:5-6 2 Peter 3:18

You come near to Me through grace. My grace is far greater than all your shortcomings, so remain under it. Out of My grace you were chosen to enter My rest, and you are restored by trusting in My amazing grace.
Grace is My strength in your weakness. Be a faithful steward of this gift, ministering in and through the grace that delivers and saves. Treasure it as your greatest possession, for My grace blesses you daily—become well acquainted with it.

September 14

Your Request

So Jesus answered and said to them,
"Assuredly, I say to you, if you have faith and do not doubt,
you will not only do what was done to the fig tree,
but also if you say to this mountain, '
Be removed and be cast into the sea,' it will be done.
And whatever things you ask in prayer, believing, you will receive."
—*Matthew 21:21-22 (NKJV)*

See also: Esther 8:4-13   1 John 5:15   1 Peter 2:9

I have chosen you—you are royal by My decree. I sought you out from among many to tell you that you have found My favor. Like Esther, I have placed the royal crown of My approval upon your head.

I see you standing quietly before Me, within My gaze, wondering, *"What will He say to my request?"* Here is the scepter I hold out to you so that you may come near and touch it. Come closer now, in confidence, and ask what you will.

In this moment, I say to you: you are more to Me than any other. You are the one I love—My crowned bride, whom My heart cannot deny. Ask Me now what you desire, and I will give you more than you have imagined—far above all you dare to ask.

September 15

Nesting

Therefore I say to you, do not worry about your life, what you will eat or what you will drink; nor about your body, what you will put on. Is not life more than food and the body more than clothing?
Look at the birds of the air, for they neither sow nor reap nor gather into barns; yet your heavenly Father feeds them. Are you not of more value than they?
— *Matthew 6:25–26 (NKJV)*

See also: Psalm 84:1-7

Like a bird in its nest, rest in My keeping power.
Rest in My ability to guard you and keep you each day.
You are My concern. Remain in My care,
and all will be well with your soul.
Do not flutter in fear when the winds rise, for I shelter you beneath My wings.
Even in the storm, your peace is found in nesting near My heart.

September 16

Every Morning

My voice You shall hear in the morning, O Lord; In the morning I will direct it to You, And I will look up.
—*Psalm 5:3 (NKJV)*

See also: Lamentations 3:23   Matthew 6:34   2 Corinthians 3:18

Good morning, beloved! Today is unlike any other, for it is filled with new things I have prepared for you to walk in. Like the dawn breaking over the horizon, let My glory awaken within your heart.

I come today to make Myself known to you afresh. I have prepared for you a newness of heart and spirit unlike yesterday's. My will is accomplished day by day, and you are a spirit ever renewed by My Spirit.

This day is as important to Me as your life itself, for today carries the unfolding of your destiny.

September 17

My Spirit Comes

If you then, being evil, know how to give good gifts to your children, how much more will your heavenly Father give the Holy Spirit to those who ask Him!
— *Luke 11:13 (NKJV)*

See also: Luke 11:9-11

I Am a good Father who gives My Spirit to all who seek, ask, and knock. Be steadfast and faithful in your pursuit of more of Me. I will not withhold Myself from those who ask. Keep on asking until My Spirit comes and pours out in full measure upon you. Ask that My Spirit rest upon you and fill you completely.

The flesh profits nothing—it is beggarly and weak. Rejoice always in surrender to My Spirit, for where My Spirit dwells, the enemy is driven out.

September 18

No Walls

> So the people shouted when the priests blew the trumpets. And it happened when the people heard the sound of the trumpet, and the people shouted with a great shout, that the wall fell down flat. Then the people went up into the city, every man straight before him, and they took the city.
> —*Joshua 6:20 (NKJV)*

See also: Psalm 139:23-24   Proverbs 4:23   1 John 3:20-21

My child, do you see the walls in your heart? They are every fear, doubt, and contrary thought that does not agree with My Word or My Spirit. I long to walk with you, talk with you, and be with you every moment. This can only happen as you purposefully tear down every wall.

Look deeply into your heart to see what I Am seeing, and talk with Me about your defenses. No wall can be found in My heart. The walls are in yours—walls you have built, believing they would protect you. But they only keep you from My very best.

Trust Me to show you what separates us. Every wall I expose in truth will fall, just as the walls of Jericho came down.

September 19

Travail

Turn your eyes away from me, For they have overcome me. Your hair is like a flock of goats Going down from Gilead.
—*Song of Songs 6:5 (NKJV)*

See also: Isaiah 61:10-11   Jeremiah 33:11   Matthew 9:15   Matthew 25:6

I Am in travail of soul, longing to be with you, My Bride. You have fasted out of your desire for Me, for though we are one in spirit, we are separated by the veil of time for now. Hear the voice of the Bridegroom calling for His Bride. Until I come, be devoted to Me and prepared to meet Me. I can hardly wait to lift the veil that hides your face and keeps you from seeing Me clearly. With just one look from your eyes, all that stands between us will vanish.

Look ahead to My soon coming, and let your thoughts dwell on the joy of our wedding day.

September 20

A Prepared Path

Lift up your heads, O you gates! And be lifted up, you everlasting doors! And the King of glory shall come in.
—*Psalm 24:7 (NKJV)*

See also: Isaiah 57:14   Matthew 3:3   John 20:27   1 John 1:1

Clear the path, for the time has come to do great exploits for your God. Let nothing hinder you—put away doubt and fear. As I told Thomas, *"Reach out your hand and touch My wounds."* Look upon Me and see the price I paid for your freedom.

I will give power to those who believe that they shall overcome. Gather up every stone in your path and remove it, for the King of Glory is coming! Plow the ground and make way for the harvest. I desire a people perfectly prepared, ready for My return.

September 21

Heaven's Witness

Not that I have already attained, or am already perfected; but I press on, that I may lay hold of that for which Christ Jesus has also laid hold of me. Brethren, I do not count myself to have apprehended; but one thing I do, forgetting those things which are behind and reaching forward to those things which are ahead.
—*Philippians 3:12-13 (NKJV)*

See also: 1 Corinthians 9:24-25   2 Timothy 4:7-8   Hebrews 12:1

There are many who have gone before you—watching and cheering you on. Heaven is like an arena filled with a great cloud of witnesses who rise to applaud every victory you win.

This heavenly crowd breaks forth in praise, celebrating each triumph of faith. Heaven rejoices with you and anticipates your next accomplishment in the Kingdom. Your perseverance stirs the atmosphere of heaven itself.

Much like a board game, you are My playing piece, moved forward as you give Me permission to act on your behalf, even in the face of opposition. Know that heaven is winning with you in this divine "game." You move heaven and earth as you press on to win the prize. The witnesses of heaven are sharing in your journey as My glory unfolds through you.

September 22

Sleeping Beauty

Like a lily among thorns, So is my love among the daughters.
—*Song of Songs 2:2 (NKJV)*

See also: Matthew 22:4-8   Romans 13:11   1 Thessalonians 5:6

In My love, you are fully alive. Now My Spirit comes as a kiss to awaken the beauty within your soul. This is the hour for your beauty to be revealed in the Kingdom.

You, My lily, have grown among thorns—in hard places, with little comfort or rest to satisfy your longing heart. Yet I call you to trust Me completely, even in the face of danger.

I Am the voice of Love that you hear, saying, *"Awake, My Bride! All is ready and prepared."*

September 23

Remember Who You Are

And suddenly a voice came from heaven, saying, "This is My beloved Son, in whom I am well pleased."
—*Matthew 3:17 (NKJV)*

See also: Matthew 4:11   Romans 6:4   2 Peter 1:17

I have baptized you into the river of Life that flows with My love. Remember Jesus, and look to see the heavens open and the dove of My Spirit descending as I declare, *"You are My beloved child, in whom I Am well pleased."*

When you are tested by the enemy, remember that you have been raised into newness of life—your old nature is dead and buried. Declare to your adversary, *"I am My Beloved's, and He is well pleased with me."*

Let your baptism into My Son make you strong against the taunts of the devil. When you remember who you are, you will no longer feel the need to prove yourself. Stand firm in your identity, and I will send ministering angels to strengthen you.

September 24

The Now Kingdom

And as you go, preach, saying, 'The kingdom of heaven is at hand.'
—Matthew 10:7 (NKJV)

See also: Matthew 16:19   Matthew 24:14   1 Peter 2:9

Rise up and take authority over your enemy in every situation through the power of My Name. I have called you into battle and strengthened you for conquest. Heaven's kingdom government is yours!
You are a child of light, making a difference wherever you go, for you carry My presence. You were not rescued merely for salvation's sake—you were transferred from the kingdom of darkness into the Kingdom of Light.
When My Kingdom is established upon the earth, then the end will come. Proclaim My message, for it has never changed.

September 25

The Bridegroom

For your Maker is your husband,
The Lord of hosts is His name,
And your Redeemer is the Holy One of Israel,
He is called the God of the whole earth.
— *Isaiah 54:5 (NKJV)*

See also: Psalm 19:1-6   Matthew 9:15   2 Corinthians 4:6

The sun that rises and moves across the earth declares from the heavens that I Am the Faithful and Glorious One. I Am the Sun of Righteousness, full of light, coming daily from My chambers—rejoicing and fulfilling My purpose: to bring light to the world and make darkness flee.

This very act of creation reveals My Son as the Bridegroom, full of glory and power to drive out darkness from the earth. The Light of the world came to dispel every shadow.

You are to declare My glory and shine through the night, for you are the light that pierces the darkness. You reflect My glory in the light of the Son each day. As surely as the dawn proclaims My majesty, My radiance is seen in your life. Watch for Me and pledge your love by waiting for My return.

September 26

Shush!

Why are you cast down, O my soul? And why are you disquieted within me? Hope in God; For I shall yet praise Him, The help of my countenance and my God.
—*Psalm 42:11 (NKJV)*

See also: Psalm 105:5   Isaiah 30:15   Mark 4:39

You have asked Me to speak to you about your distress, but you have not quieted your soul.
Say over yourself, *"Be still."*
When your soul becomes quiet, you will hear Me speaking over you, *"Peace, be still."*
In My peace, you overcome every fear and every despairing thought.
Here, in quietness and rest, you know Me best.
Recount all that I have done for you, and let gratitude guard your heart.

September 27

God Calling

My beloved spoke, and said to me: "Rise up, my love, my fair one, And come away."
—Song of Songs 2:10 (NKJV)

See also: Isaiah 44:8   1 Corinthians 2:13   2 Corinthians 12:9

The flesh profits little, especially in times of pain or hurt. Your one need is to look away—to My Spirit. I have given you My Holy Spirit to lift you above all that is in this world.

Do not look to your soul, for emotions are fleeting. Look to Me, for I Am the Solid Rock of all ages. You will make spiritual progress upon every truth I have revealed to you in worship.

Confess your weaknesses, but do not dwell on them. Look higher—My glory will overcome every frailty in your mind. Come away, My beloved; I long to share with you the joy of My presence.

September 28

My One and Only

If I should count them, they would be more in number than the sand;
When I awake, I am still with You.
—*Psalm 139:18 (NKJV)*

See also: Isaiah 43:7   2 Corinthians 5:17

My love for you is without measure. Know that you are precious in My sight, and do not let your thoughts place you among the many. You are not a speck in the sand but a light in a dark world—a bright star shining for Me as you carry My glory wherever you go.

Before you were conceived, it was My pleasure to plan every detail of your being. You are Mine by design, and you are also Mine by the blood of My Son, who redeemed you to walk with Me in everlasting love.

My one and only.

September 29

Declare It!

And Jabez called on the God of Israel saying, "Oh, that You would bless me indeed, and enlarge my territory, that Your hand would be with me, and that You would keep me from evil, that I may not cause pain!" So God granted him what he requested.
—*1 Chronicles 4:10 (NKJV)*

See also: Job 22:28   Psalm 51:15

I am God's artist.
I will use my talent to reveal His glory to the world.
I will uncover deep things hidden in His heart.
I will light up the night with images from heaven.
I will dream bigger dreams for His Name's sake.
I will influence the world and take back territory for God.

September 30

Powerful Peace

Peace I leave with you, My peace I give to you; not as the world gives do I give to you. Let not your heart be troubled, neither let it be afraid.
—*John 14:27 (NKJV)*

See also: John 16:33   John 20:26   Romans 16:20

My dear child, I made you to abide in Me; therefore, I have placed My peace within your very DNA. It is My peace your body and soul crave. My perfect peace is always available—greater than any circumstance you face.

Do not let the world around you steal this peace. Without it, your heart can grow weary of life. Step out of the world's turmoil and linger a little longer in My presence. Here your mind is renewed, and your whole being made complete.

Desire peace and pursue it, for peace will preserve both your body and soul. My peace is the perfect solution for this world's troubles. Stand firm in it, and you will crush Satan under your feet.

All That I Am

October 1

Remember

**The Lord is good to all,
And His tender mercies are over all His works.**
— *Psalm 145:9 (NKJV)*

See also: Psalm 103:2   Psalm 143:5   Galatians 3:14

I have gone before you to make your way victorious in every circumstance through My blessings. Be careful to look for Me in all that I have done. I Am the God of Abraham, Isaac, and Jacob—the One who helps you.
See how greatly I have blessed you, and do not forget all My benefits. Look and recognize My hand upon your life. Build Me an altar and worship Me for all that I have done. Looking to the past thusly will establish your tomorrows.

October 2

Moving Ahead

> But those who wait on the LORD
> Shall renew *their* strength;
> They shall mount up with wings like eagles,
> They shall run and not be weary,
> They shall walk and not faint.
> — *Isaiah 40:31 (NKJV)*

See also: Psalm 145:13   Matthew 11:29

I Am moving you forward for My Kingdom's sake, ordaining you to accomplish the tasks I have given you—not in your own strength, but in Mine.

I will be with you and instruct you as you go.

Trust Me, and do not try to figure out how you will manage as you move ahead.

Let Me make the impossible easy as you walk with Me by faith and follow My ways.

October 3

In My Name

For You, Lord, have made me glad through Your work; I will triumph in the works of Your hands.
—Psalm 92:4 (NKJV)

See also: Proverbs 16:3   Ephesians 2:10

I Am always at work in your life.
The things you consider small are, to Me, great works.
Take joy in all that I do.
Create each day in My strength.
I have chosen you to be a blessing and to bring honor to My Name.
Do all in My Name.

October 4

Words of Life

It is the Spirit who gives life; the flesh profits nothing. The words that I speak to you are spirit, and they are life.
—John 6:63 (NKJV)

I Am the food of heaven; you must gather enough of Me to sustain your life today.

The manna you gathered yesterday will not be enough for you now. That is why I said, *"Give us this day our daily bread."*

Apply this truth to your life and you will live, for the words I speak to you are Spirit and they are Life.

It is My Spirit that produces life within you, My power restoring your soul. You are made alive in Me as I speak to you daily.

October 5

I See You

> Then she called the name of the Lord who spoke to her, You-Are-the-God-Who-Sees; for she said, "Have I also here seen Him who sees me?"
> —*Genesis 16:13 (NKJV)*

See also: Ephesians 1:4   Ephesians 5:8   1 Peter 2:9

See, you are accepted in My love.
I see you clothed in My righteousness, as with a robe.
See yourself in My presence—blameless.
I see you transferred into My Kingdom of light.
I see you wearing the crown I have given you.
I see you bringing others near to My throne room.
I see your life as a declaration of all My goodness and faithfulness in your generation.

October 6

Hide and Seek

> He also brought me out into a broad place; He delivered me because He delighted in me.
> —*Psalm 18:19 (NKJV)*

See also: Psalm 40:16   Proverbs 8:17   Jeremiah 9:24   Hebrews 2:13

I see you playfully close to Me, looking up to see if I notice you at My feet. I Am calling you to come even closer and take hold of Me, for I Am taking hold of you.

Your gaze is what I long for; your face is what I love to see. I have made many beautiful things, but you are one of My most delightful creations. When you look for Me, I Am delighted. When you turn to be sure I Am near, know that I Am smiling over you.

Take joy in knowing that you are becoming a most delightful heir of Mine. Continue in this beautiful game of seeking Me, and I will find you. Say to Me, *"Here I am, Father,"* and I will always come for you and draw you to Myself.

October 7

Born Royal

I will instruct you and teach you in the way you should go; I will guide you with My eye.
—*Psalm 32:8 (NKJV)*

See also: Isaiah 62:3   John 14:26   Galatians 4:7

We are a Royal Family! You are a celebrity in My Kingdom, and I want you to know that you are the light shining into the darkness of this world. It is you, My star.

Let My Word parent and delight you daily. You will not grow weak in body or soul, for every morning I instruct and encourage you. I Am the Great Communicator—always available to you. I delight in your joy to be with Me. You are important in My Kingdom, and I wait for you to walk fully into your destiny, for destiny is yours by royal birth. You are called to rule and reign with Me. I Am giving you more responsibility because I know you will return My love and work with Me.

Keep pressing on to know whose you are. You are My heir in a Kingdom where dreams come true.

October 8

New Faith

You have heard; See all this. And will you not declare it? I have made you hear new things from this time, Even hidden things, and you did not know them.
—*Isaiah 48:6 (NKJV)*

See also: John 16:13   1 Corinthians 2:7-16

It is to you that I reveal the things that are Mine, and I transmit them to you, for you are greatly loved in the Son. It is by and through My Spirit—who searches and explores all that is Mine, even the bottomless depths of My counsel—that you receive these truths.

These are My very thoughts, freely given to you, for you have the mind of Christ. Some of what I desire to reveal is beyond your present comprehension, for I Am calling you to new heights of faith.

October 9

My Family

God sets the solitary in families; He brings out those who are bound into prosperity; But the rebellious dwell in a dry land.
—*Psalm 68:6 (NKJV)*

See also: Matthew 12:50   John 15:14-15

You know Me as Savior, for I have paid the price for your redemption. I have brought you to Myself through My own blood. I took on your identity to pay the debt you owed.

Now you are Mine—brought near as an heir, My beloved. You are My brother, My sister, joined with Me in relationship to our Father.

October 10

Lasting Joy

The grass withers, the flower fades,
But the word of our God stands forever.
—*Isaiah 40:8 (NKJV)*

See also: John 12:25   2 Corinthians 4:18   Hebrews 10:34

Rejoice in eternity, for eternity is real and everlasting.
All else is fading away!
Set your eyes on what cannot be shaken, for My Kingdom endures forever. The things of this world are passing shadows, but what I have prepared for you is glorious and unending. Let your heart find joy in the eternal, for you already belong to forever.

October 11

In My Faithfulness

Behold, the Lord's hand is not shortened, That it cannot save; Nor His ear heavy, That it cannot hear.
—*Isaiah 59:1 (NKJV)*

See also: 2 Timothy 2:11-13

Out of My faithfulness, you have been lifted from the pit where you once fell and set upon the upward path you now walk. When your faith wavers, remind yourself of all that I have done.

Rejoice, for My hand is always reaching down to rescue you. Now let My faithfulness be your confidence.

October 12

My Dear Children

**But Jesus said,
Let the little children come to Me, and do not forbid them,
for of such is the kingdom of heaven.**
— *Matthew 19:14 (NKJV)*

See also: Romans 8:14-16   Ephesians 5:8   1 John 2:14

Do not forget to be free in spirit, for I Am not requiring anything of you. You were made for My pleasure, just as I Am meant to be your soul's delight. Ask Me for My opinion first, rather than seeking your own or another's. You are My child—be willing to hear and willing to ask, for then you will truly know Me as your Father.
I Am longing for your childlike trust and love, for these are the foundation of My Kingdom. You are accepted, so come to Me quickly and eagerly, without pretense or concern of your own making.
I Am your Abba. You are My child, born of My divine nature and forever before Me in love.

October 13

The Power of Forgiveness

"Come now, and let us reason together," Says the Lord, "Though your sins are like scarlet, They shall be as white as snow; Though they are red like crimson, They shall be as wool."
—*Isaiah 1:18 (NKJV)*

See also: Isaiah 61:1   Matthew 18:22-35   1 Peter 1:18-19

My forgiveness brings life and freedom. I alone remove your sentence of shame, guilt, and condemnation—those filthy, bloodstained rags—and replace them with a robe of pure white.

My blood is the cleansing soap of heaven, washing away every stain of your past. But you must also apply this blood to your own heart by releasing everyone you have imprisoned through unforgiveness.

Free them, forgive them, and I will free you also. Your own freedom depends on those you are still holding hostage. Apply My blood to the doorposts of your heart and let go of every debt that I Myself have already paid for. Your freedom is at stake.

October 14

Trials and Testing

But this He said to test him, for He Himself knew what He would do
—John 6:6 (NKJV)

See also: Jeremiah 17:10   Jeremiah 20:12   Zechariah 13:9

Before I trust you with greater assignments, I allow decisions to rise that reveal what you cannot yet see. These moments uncover blind spots and weaknesses so they can be strengthened, not so you can be shamed. I refine you so that you do not become a stumbling block to others. Every choice becomes a classroom, every decision an invitation to grow in My wisdom. Learn well. Step forward. Pass your test.

October 15

The Key

But blessed are your eyes for they see, and your ears for they hear; for assuredly, I say to you that many prophets and righteous men desired to see what you see, and did not see it, and to hear what you hear, and did not hear it.
—*Matthew 13:16-17 (NKJV)*

See also: John 10:7-9   John 10:27   Revelation 3:7

I Am the Gate that leads into green pastures, and there is no other entrance. In My pasture, there is peace, for the water of My Spirit flows freely in the presence of My glory.

I have given you ears to hear what the Spirit is saying and eyes to see what others cannot see. These are the days of Elijah—days of preparation for My soon coming.

Follow Me with all your heart, and do not be dull of hearing. I hold the key that unlocks every door.

October 16

Glory Days

He has shown you, O man, what is good, and what does the Lord require of you but to do justly, to love mercy, and to walk humbly with your God.
—*Micah 6:8 (NKJV)*

Glory in knowing Me personally and practically.
Glory in hearing My voice.
Glory in dwelling in My presence.
Glory in discerning and knowing My character.
Glory in trusting My timing and resting in My will.
Glory in seeing My hand move through the ordinary.
Glory in walking in My truth and reflecting My love.
Glory in carrying My name with joy before the world.

October 17

Presence and Sincerity

Examine me, O Lord, and prove me; Try my mind and my heart.
—*Psalm 26:2 (NKJV)*

See also: John 8:36

Live before Me carefully, seeking always to please Me—even when the choice is hard. I Am your guide, so be willing to lay down your own reputation for Mine.

Many have stumbled in hypocrisy as they led others, so check your course often, for I Am your true North. I will free you from all pretense when you walk in true liberty, refusing to yield to the flesh or to your old ways of doing things for Me.

Walk with Me in sincerity, free from the bondage of seeking the approval of others. Let My endorsement be all that you require.

October 18

Keep On

Seek the Lord and His strength, seek His face evermore.
—*Psalm 105:4 (NKJV)*

See also: 1 John 3:22   Hebrews 11:6

My beloved, My arms are outstretched before you, laying down handfuls on purpose out of My concern for your well-being. In knowing this, keep seeking My face, for I desire for you to know Me deeply.

My thoughts and My plans for you are like hidden treasure. You must seek Me to uncover all that I have prepared for you and draw from My strength for your life. Do not despair, even for a moment, for I Am a good, good Father who gives you what you need in due time.

Keep seeking Me, even when you fear that you have failed. I will never disapprove of you, for My love for you is complete and unending.

October 19

Salvation Is...

Fear not, for I am with you; Be not dismayed, for I am your God. I will strengthen you, Yes, I will help you, I will uphold you with My righteous right hand.
—*Isaiah 41:10 (NKJV)*

I Am your safety in every trial, in weakness, and in pain.
I hold you close to My heart and will never release the hand that reaches for Me.
When fear rises, remember that I Am your shelter and the covering over your life.
Rest beneath My wings, for no storm can break through My love for you.
I Am your stronghold and your peace in the midst of chaos.
You are safe in Me—now and always.

October 20

Before Me

> Therefore let us not judge one another anymore, but rather resolve this, not to put a stumbling block or a cause to fall in our brother's way.
> —*Romans 14:13 (NKJV)*

See also: Colossians 3:12-13   1 Peter 5:5

You do not see your own nakedness without the help of another. Some, when confronted with their own lack, try to cover themselves with feigned modesty, never truly admitting their inadequacies. They do not see their need.

Others judge you and speak opinions that do not help but only hinder, for they see only the outward appearance. Clothe yourself instead with humility, love, and mercy.

Look for My approval first, then listen to another's evaluation with an open heart. Afterward, come to Me again and ask what I think, for only My perspective brings truth and freedom.

October 21

The Beauty of a Woman

> Then the rib which the Lord God had taken from man He made into a woman, and He brought her to the man. And Adam said:
> "This is now bone of my bones
> And flesh of my flesh;
> She shall be called Woman,
> Because she was taken out of Man."
> —*Genesis 2:22-23 (NKJV)*

See also: Psalm 8:5   Psalm 45:11-14

The first woman was created in glory—the work of My artistry, beautiful to behold.

Like her, My daughter, you are clothed in My beauty. Your garments are the white robes of My forgiveness, a beauty of innocence purchased by the Lamb who was slain.

See the crown of gold that I place upon your head. This adornment is given so that you may stand tall and behold what I have done to make you altogether lovely.

You are My royal daughter, and even the angels look in wonder at your beauty. Begin to see yourself as I see you.

October 22

In My Keeping

> O Jerusalem, Jerusalem, the one who kills the prophets and stones those who are sent to her! How often I wanted to gather your children together, as a hen *gathers* her brood under *her* wings, but you were not willing!
> —*Luke 13:34 (NKJV)*

See also: Psalm 91:1-4   Isaiah 30:15

Let Me gather you under the shelter of My wings, where you are safe. Remind yourself who I Am to you—your Father. Out of My faithfulness and the promises I have spoken over you, raise up a shield of truth over your mind. Settle yourself in confident hope. Do not fear anything the enemy is doing to cause you distress. Choose to see Me as your God—forever Almighty, ready and willing to save.

When you grow quiet and rest in Me, you will see with your own eyes the dawning of a new beginning upon your life.

October 23

Modesty for Today

Then the eyes of both of them were opened, and they knew that they were naked; and they sewed fig leaves together and made themselves coverings. And they heard the sound of the Lord God walking in the garden in the cool of the day, and Adam and his wife hid themselves from the presence of the Lord God among the trees of the garden.
—*Genesis 3:7-8 (NKJV)*

See also: 1 Peter 2:3-4

Leave behind your fig leaves and let My righteousness clothe you fully. Look into the mirror with Me, seeking only My approval. I have asked you not to be competitive or vainglorious, for I despise pride.

I delight in the beauty I have bestowed upon you. Be satisfied in knowing how I see you. Immodesty is demonic in nature and leads many into impurity. Be selfless in how you present yourself, surrendering even this area of weakness to Me. You are meant to stand out—not in vanity, but as a bright light shining in the darkness.

October 24

The Shepherd's Song

He will feed His flock like a shepherd; He will gather the lambs with His arm, And carry them in His bosom, And gently lead those who are with young.
—Isaiah 40:11 (NKJV)

See also: John 10:2-7   1 Peter 2:25

This is the melody I Am singing over your life. I Am the Shepherd who cares for you like no other. You are constantly under My watchful eye, and I have promised that you will lack nothing.
I Am the Door into the sheepfold, protecting and shielding you daily from danger, for I Am near. We are abiding together—so lie down in peace.
Know that I Am tending to your life so you may flourish. Rest in My goodness, for I Am the Good Shepherd.

October 25

Purity

Who may ascend into the hill of the Lord? Or who may stand in His holy place?
—*Psalm 24:3 (NKJV)*

See also: Psalm 103:17-18   Jeremiah 9:24

Enter into a covenant with Me—an agreement that cuts away everything that is not of Me.
I desire to make you My personal possession, set apart and wholly Mine.
Allow Me to write My laws upon your heart, for this covenant is sealed not with ink, but with My Spirit.
Let the old fall away, for I Am making all things new within you.
Walk before Me in holiness and know that I Am yours, and you are Mine forever.

October 26

Good God

And he said, Please, show me Your glory.
— *Exodus 33:18 (NKJV)*

See also: Psalm 31:19   Psalm 107:1

Your Goodness, God
Delicious—a taste from above, the dessert that fills my cup.
You are intentional; You know who I am, placing Your goodness, like a treat, into my hand.
Good things are in Your plan.
I am content, for Your love covers me like a blanket—it comforts and cheers.
It is Your guarantee that I will never fear.
Evil will not overtake nor come near to me.
In Your protection I am unmoved—a fortress over my heart and life.
Your goodness, like a fountain, flows into me.
Yes! I smile at the days to come.

October 27

My Love

Keep yourselves in the love of God, looking for the mercy of our Lord Jesus Christ unto eternal life.
—Jude 1:21 (NKJV)

Check your level of love, little child of Mine.
Keep yourself in My love, for this is your abiding place—where you will know Me and receive from Me.
Love is the constant theme of heaven, so hold fast to your love for Me.
Never let it fade, even for a moment, for love is the flame that keeps your heart alive in My presence.

October 28

Remain In Me

**But the Lord is in His holy temple.
Let all the earth keep silence before Him.**
— *Habakkuk 2:20 (NKJV)*

See also: Song of Songs 2:10   Hebrews 2:3

Take time to simply be with Me in quietness, and I will come and be with you.
Anticipate My presence, for what I Am giving you in these moments is My very Self—something that adds to your life what can never be taken away.
To see and hear with Me is true spiritual food from heaven that does not deceive, for I have come to dwell with you.
This is abiding—here you learn to remain in Me and with Me. How will you know Me in any other way?
Contemplate every word I speak to you, and do not neglect so great a salvation. I will give you a deeper, more personal knowledge of Me, for I delight in you.

October 29

Trust as You Go

> But may the God of all grace, who called us to His eternal glory by Christ Jesus, after you have suffered a while, perfect, establish, strengthen, and settle you.
> —*1 Peter 5:10 (NKJV)*

See also: 2 Thessalonians 3:13   Job 20:12   Psalm 27:11-14

Hold back your tongue and do not argue with others, for I Am contending for you.
Let your trust rest in Me, for I will deliver you from all opposition.
Stand before Me innocent and upright, free from presumptuous sin, for you are meant to bring joy to My heart.
Look for the good in every situation, and you will find the courage to walk into the unknown as I lead you.
No one else can fulfill what I have entrusted to you.
Accept your assignment, and I will strengthen you for the task ahead.

October 30

Freedom Reigns

Now the Lord is the Spirit, and where the Spirit of the Lord is, there is liberty.
—2 Corinthians 3:17 (NKJV)

See also: Isaiah 61:1-2   Romans 8:15   2 Corinthians 5:17

You were born again to fly free—free to love Me and to love others,
free from all that binds you to the earthly, free from everything that hinders and separates us.
Freedom is where your soul soars to new heights.
Let **"Freedom!"** be your battle cry, for I have called you to reign in My Kingdom.

October 31
The Force of Love

Nor height nor depth, nor any other created thing, shall be able to separate us from the love of God which is in Christ Jesus our Lord.
—*Romans 8:39 (NKJV)*

See also: 1 Corinthians 13:13

The greatest force in the universe is Love.
My love is the conquering power that changes the world around you.
Become acquainted with My love, and watch as I transform you from within.
Let My love rule in all your dealings with others, and I will work mightily on your behalf.
Love is the most powerful force—it is Me.

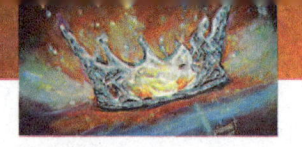

November

November 1

Pray

When You said, "Seek My face," My heart said to You, "Your face, Lord, I will seek."
—Psalm 27:8 (NKJV)

See also: Matthew 14:23   John 14:27

Never discount a single prayer, for every whisper moves heaven.
Be in the eternal realm by bowing low.
Seek the heavenly and not the fleeting.
Why wait for an opportune time? Just do it.
We are one as we meet and talk.
As we meet, I will give peace to your soul.

November 2

Heaven's Glory

> To them God willed to make known what are the riches of the glory of this mystery among the Gentiles: which is Christ in you, the hope of glory.
> —*Colossians 1:27 (NKJV)*

See also: 2 Corinthians 3:9-18   2 Corinthians 4:17-18

Think on the things that are glorious. Set your thoughts on My thoughts toward you, for here in heaven truth resides. To be My ambassador, you must become familiar with our dwelling so you can represent My Kingdom well on the earth. Walk on higher ground, for I long to reveal more of heaven to those who turn from darkness to see heaven's light. Walk with Me into the light of glory, and you will bring My glory down to the earth.

November 3

To My Child

He who glories, let him glory in the Lord.
—1 Corinthians 1:31 (NKJV)

See also: 1 John 3:1   1 John 4:16-17

My little child, you are filled with My joy, for the Light has dawned as you walk in the light of My fellowship.

You are learning to know and understand Me, through your own observation and the experiences we share together.

Rejoice, My child, for the victory has been given to you—by faith, you overcome this world.

November 4

Authority and Power

And Jesus came and spoke to them, saying, "All authority has been given to Me in heaven and on earth. Go therefore and make disciples of all the nations, baptizing them in the name of the Father and of the Son and of the Holy Spirit, teaching them to observe all things that I have commanded you; and lo, I am with you always, even to the end of the age." Amen.
—*Matthew 28:18-20 (NKJV)*

See also: Mark 16:17-20   1 Corinthians 4:20

My Word empowers you to do all that I have spoken.
My life was given for the cause of victory.
Rise up and declare that you are strong in My strength.
Use the resurrection power within you—begin today and believe what I have already given.
Do not say you believe if you do not use what I have entrusted to you.
Repent, and take your rightful position in the Kingdom I paid for.
"It is finished" was the declaration to your enemy.
I purchased power and authority for My glory.

November 5

Give What You Have

"Give, and it will be given to you: good measure, pressed down, shaken together, and running over will be put into your bosom, For with the same measure that you use, it will be measured back to you."
—*Luke 6:38 (NKJV)*

See also: Matthew 10:8

Learn to give what I have placed within you. What I have entrusted to you is not for you alone, but for the sake of others. As you pour out, you create room for more. Look for opportunities to draw from your own storehouse, even if all you can offer is a cup, and you will become a well of refreshment that I will continually fill from heaven. Give freely, for I Am seeking every opportunity to bless you as you make room for more.

November 6

God's Words

> For you have been born again, not of perishable seed, but of the imperishable, through the living and enduring word of God.
> —*1 Peter 1:23 (NKJV)*

See also: Matthew 17:5   John 4:10   John 10:3

Look back through time and see this truth, from My spoken word comes an immediate, life-giving response that changes the world. My written word is the foundation of all I have done and all I will do for you. My Word, spoken, is the fountain of living water I promised, flowing deep and freely into your life moment by moment.

I want you to hear My voice and not remain deaf, to see My word and not remain blind.

I Am near to you. I Am the living Word, and My words are life and life-giving. My people will not be bound by dead orthodoxy, but will come to a flowing fountain.

You do not need to study, strive, or search for the Bread of Life, for you shall partake of it. It comes down to you and is given as you live by every word.

November 7

Love!

Love suffers long and is kind; love does not envy; love does not parade itself, is not puffed up; does not behave rudely, does not seek its own, is not provoked, thinks no evil.
—1 Corinthians 13:4–5 (NKJV)

See also: 1 Corinthians Chapter 13   1 John 4:7–8

My love chooses kindness and patience.
It has no need to prove itself or to be right.
My love sees through deception and remains steady.
It does not let feelings lead but follows the truth.
My love is intentional.
It thinks of others first and examines the motives of the heart.

November 8

My Pleasure

Therefore the Lord God of Israel says: "I said indeed that your house and the house of your father would walk before Me forever." But now the Lord says: "Far be it from Me; for those who honor Me I will honor, and those who despise Me shall be lightly esteemed."
—1 Samuel 2:30 (NKJV)

See also: Psalm 139:16   Psalm 144:3

I have written down all the days of your life and keep them before Me.
Order your steps in My direction above all else, for I honor those who honor Me.
I take great pleasure in caring for you.
Trust that nothing escapes My notice, for every detail has purpose in My plan.
Walk in confidence, knowing that My delight in you will sustain your every step.

November 9

Holy and Whole

Beloved, I pray that you may prosper in all things and be in health, just as your soul prospers.
—3 John 1:2 (NKJV)

See also: 1 Thessalonians 5:23   1 Peter 1:16

I Am concerned with your wholeness—body, soul, and spirit.
When you are whole, you reflect more of who I Am.
Can you mirror My nature if your heart or mind is sick?
I desire you restored and complete, for in that place you will accomplish much for My Kingdom.
Wholeness is not the absence of struggle but the presence of My healing power within you.
Let My Spirit touch every part of your being until nothing remains fractured or forgotten.

November 10

I Am Truth

**For I rejoiced greatly when brethren came and testified of the truth that is in you,
just as you walk in the truth.
I have no greater joy than to hear that my children walk in truth.**
—*3 John 1:3-4 (NKJV)*

See also: John 8:32   John 14:17   John 18:37

I Am with those who seek Me with sincerity because I dwell in truth. You recognize My presence in the steady whisper that keeps you aligned with honesty. Truth is sincere and pure, and it has the strength to hold you steady on any mission. It hates injustice, loves peace, and extends mercy while standing as a sword against evil. My truth brings life to others and sets you apart as holy. You will find truth in My Word, not in the opinions of others or your own. Truth must be pursued because it carries the reward of living close to Me. This is why I came to bear witness to the truth.

November 11

Light and Life

The entrance of Your words gives light;
It gives understanding to the simple.
—Psalm 119:130 (NKJV)

See also: Isaiah 60:1-2   Matthew 5:14-16   John 8:12

I search your heart, so take care to walk in the light of all that I show you.
What I reveal is for our companionship and for My glory to shine through your life.
My light exposes truth and drives out every lie, bringing you into newness of life and joy.
Come into the Light, My beloved, and let My radiance make you whole.

November 12

Seek, Ask, and Find

Trust in the Lord with all your heart,
And lean not on your own understanding.
In all your ways acknowledge Him,
And He shall direct your paths.
—*Proverbs 3:5–6 (NKJV)*

See also: 1 Corinthians 2:10-16   1 Corinthians 4:5-6

Teach purity, honor, and unadulterated truth.
Instruct in all that is right so that none will stumble.
My Spirit speaks to reveal righteousness to My Body, not condemnation, for judgment is reserved for the unbelieving.
I Am the One who uncovers the secret motives and intentions of the heart.
Seek, ask, and find Me, for I Am Wisdom, and I Am Truth.
Those who search for Me with a sincere heart will uncover treasures hidden since the beginning.

November 13

Serving Low, Rising High

> But when you are invited, go and sit down in the lowest place, so that when he who invited you comes he may say to you, 'Friend, go up higher.' Then you will have glory in the presence of those who sit at the table with you.
> —*Luke 14:10 (NKJV)*

See also: John 13:14-17   John 15:10-12

Look at those I have placed around you and see lives, like yours, in transformation.
All who are in Me have entered into newness of life.
Even those who seem far from My love still carry traces of the good I planted in them from the beginning.
See My children through the lens of My image, and you will see My heart.
I have commanded you to love even the least and to serve your brothers and sisters with sincerity.
Take the lower seat, and in due time I will raise you up.
Ask Me for the perfect gift of love, so that all will know you are truly My disciple—for no other can follow Me without it.

November 14

Help from On High

Happy is he who has the God of Jacob for his help, Whose hope is in the Lord his God.
—*Psalm 146:5 (NKJV)*

See also: Psalm 121:2-8

Today I Am giving you wings to lift and undergird you, helping you soar higher and steadying your steps so your foot will not slip—because you have asked for My help.
I Am giving you faith to move mountains and renewing your strength, for your hope is in Me.
I Am with you, and you will not fall.

November 15

Child of Mine

Then I will give them a heart to know Me, that I am the Lord; and they shall be My people, and I will be their God, for they shall return to Me with their whole heart.
—Jeremiah 24:7 (NKJV)

See also: John 10:29   1 John 4:18

I hold this child of yours in My hand, and I will not let go.
I know every detail, and My plans are Mine, not your own.
Do not give in to fear, for where fear rules, love and trust cannot dwell.
Release the one you love to Me, and I will accomplish far more than you could ever imagine.
I Am writing a new chapter that will soon unfold before your eyes.
Be confident in My ability to direct, guard, and shape this life that rests in My keeping.
I know the future and everything required for the transformation that is coming.
Ask Me to protect your heart with this truth, for I love you deeply and care for those you love even more.
Ask Me to place a hedge of protection around this child of Mine, and rest in the assurance of My faithfulness to you.

November 16

Seek Truth

For "who has known the mind of the Lord that he may instruct Him?"
But we have the mind of Christ.
—*1 Corinthians 2:16 (NKJV)*

See also: 2 Timothy 2:15   Proverbs 24:10

Let truth reign over all your thoughts.
Surrender Lordship to Me, and I will give you the ability to hear Truth clearly.
Your ears will hear, and your eyes will open to greater revelation.
Stand in courage, and do not let your heart be weighed down by discouragement, for I have already overcome all things.
Rise up and take your stand; do not faint in the days of adversity.
I Am with you, and I Am fighting for you.
Stand beside Me on this side of heaven, where faith sees beyond what is seen.
I Am not found in earthly striving but in the higher place of My presence.
Let Me carry you upward into deeper truth and revelation as you read My Word.

November 17

Manna and Mercy

So He humbled you, allowed you to hunger, and fed you with manna which you did not know nor did your fathers know, that He might make you know that man shall not live by bread alone; but man lives by every word that proceeds from the mouth of the Lord.
—*Deuteronomy 8:3 (NKJV)*

See also: Lamentations 3:22-23   Psalm 78:24-25   John 6:48-58

There are seasons when I allow hunger so you can see more clearly where your life truly comes from. Manna was given to teach My people that provision is not found in what they could gather, but in what came from My mouth each day. I work the same way in you.

When familiar sources no longer sustain you, do not fear. I Am drawing you back to the place where My Word becomes your daily bread. Trust Me for today's portion. As you listen and receive, you will find strength, insight, and life that no earthly supply can give. I will feed you with what is from heaven, and My mercy will meet you again each morning.

November 18

Victories

**Return to your rest, O my soul,
For the LORD has dealt bountifully with you.**
—Psalm 116:7 (NKJV)

See also: Isaiah 30:15   Matthew 11:29

It is the soul at rest that finds its victories.
Rest in Me, and you will see triumph born from stillness.
In quiet trust, My Spirit moves with power beyond your striving.
From your rest, I release strength that cannot be shaken.

November 19

Take My Comfort

"Comfort, yes, comfort My people!" Says your God.
—*Isaiah 40:1 (NKJV)*

See also: Isaiah 51:12   Isaiah 61:2-3   2 Corinthians 1:4

I Am the God of all comfort, and I have rescued you.
Turn again and strengthen another who has fallen low.
I will give you My very words to speak, for you know Me more deeply now.
Say to the downcast, "Hope is here! Lift up your eyes and look to our God—He is able to deliver you!"
Comfort those who walk the same path you once walked.
Take up this mantle, and I will use you as I used Isaiah, to bring courage to My people.
My people are aching for My comfort.
Receive My comfort like a soft mantle upon your shoulders, and then give that same comfort to those in need.

November 20

The Great Sword

For the word of God is living and powerful, sharper than any two-edged sword, piercing even to the division of soul and spirit, and of joints and marrow, and is a discerner of the thoughts and intents of the heart.
—*Hebrews 4:12 (NKJV)*

See also: Hosea 6:1-2   John 11:25   2 Corinthians 4:11-16

My Word is a great sword, piercing your heart and cutting through your mind, your will, and your emotions to bring forth this great exchange—My mind for yours.
I Am the One who takes your pierced heart and gives you Mine in return, whole and new.
Whenever you are wounded, come to Me, and I will bind your wounds with My healing presence.
Even in the moments you think you will not survive what I have allowed, I Am at work within you, exchanging My hurts, My wounds, and even My scars for your continual healing and wholeness.

November 21

My Peace

Depart from evil and do good; Seek peace and pursue it.
—Psalm 34:14 (NKJV)

See also: Isaiah 26:3   Isaiah 59:8   John 14:27   Romans 16:20

It is My peace that your body craves and your spirit longs for.
My perfect peace is yours for the asking.
The enemy and the world around you seek to steal it, for without peace the soul grows weary and the body weakens.
Do not conform to the chaos of this world.
Come away and dwell in My presence, where My perfect peace is found.
Keep your mind fixed on Me, and walk daily in the peace you have received.
My peace restores your spirit, steadies your mind, and strengthens your body.
In My peace you are preserved—body, soul, and spirit.
Abide continually in My peace, and you will stand unshaken when the world trembles.

November 22

Changing Seasons

Behold, I will do a new thing,
Now it shall spring forth;
Shall you not know it?
I will even make a road in the wilderness
And rivers in the desert.
—Isaiah 43:19 (NKJV)

See also: Ecclesiastes 3:1   1 Chronicles 12:32

You have entered a now time.
What I spoke to your heart has prepared you for these days.
Catch the gravity of what you have been given, and advance with intention and purpose.
Be deliberate and precise as you move ahead.
Be open, for I Am releasing new things in this new season.
Step when I prompt you, and you will see doors open that no one can shut.

November 23

All of Me

> If you seek her as silver,
> And search for her as for hidden treasures;
> Then you will understand the fear of the Lord,
> And find the knowledge of God.
> For the Lord gives wisdom;
> From His mouth come knowledge and understanding.
> —*Proverbs 2:4-6 (NKJV)*

See also: Luke 10:39   Colossians 2:9

I have said, Come and sit with Me.
I Am inviting you into all that I Am—your Father, your Savior, and your Comforter.
I have given you My wisdom and My counsel; now make room in your heart for all of Me.
Yes, pay attention to My Spirit's invitation, for in stillness you will hear My whisper and know My heart.

November 24

Heaven's Worship

Then David danced before the Lord with all his might; and David was wearing a linen ephod.
—2 Samuel 6:14 (NKJV)

See also: Psalm 29:2   John 4:23   Revelation 4:10-11

Come up here and enter into worship in total abandonment.
This is the bridge that carries the atmosphere of heaven to the earth.
Dance before Me as angels dance beside you.
True worship is found in surrender—when you release all of yourself to Me.
I delight in you, My beloved, as your worship rises and fills heaven with fragrance.

November 25

Out of Fear

Have I not commanded you, be strong and of good courage, do not be afraid, nor be dismayed, for the Lord your God is with you wherever you go.
—*Joshua 1:9 (NKJV)*

See also: Isaiah 44:2   Luke 12:32   2 Timothy 1:7

You are My little one, being gently pulled along by Me.
Hear Me say, "Do not fear! Come, run with Me. Take My hand!"
I Am pulling you out of fear and into freedom.
As I lead you, others will follow and take hold of your hand, drawn together into the flow of My love—out of fear and into perfect freedom.

November 26

The Cross

And I, if I am lifted up from the earth, will draw all peoples to Myself.
—*John 12:32 (NKJV)*

See also: Acts 26:18   Romans 12:5   Ephesians 2:8

The cross of Jesus stands at the crossroads of history, dividing the destiny of mankind.
It reaches down to humanity, clearing the way for all who would enter heaven's gates by God's grace.
The cross is the bond that holds the Body of Christ together, for we are united in His death and resurrection.
All who behold the cross in its splendor come to know the beauty of forgiveness and the power of redemption.
Forever the cross of Christ stands as a wonder—and everlasting life, an even greater wonder still.

November 27

Walk with Me

But Noah found grace in the eyes of the Lord.
—*Genesis 6:8 (NKJV)*

See also: Isaiah 30:21   Colossians 2:6   1 Thessalonians 5:10

Walk with Me hand in hand as My friend today.
Stay in step with Me, knowing that I give you everything you need.
I love your sweet companionship—you were created for this closeness.
Together, we will move into all that I have prepared for you, as you stay keenly aware of My nearness.
Let today be your only concern.
Walk with Me as Noah walked, and you will discover freedom from the weight of yesterday and the worry of tomorrow.
We walk together in the eternal now, where every moment is filled with My presence.

November 28

Called to the Harvest

> Then He said to them, "The harvest truly is great, but the laborers are few; therefore pray the Lord of the harvest to send out laborers into His harvest."
> —*Luke 10:2 (NKJV)*

See also: Ruth 2:16   Luke 12:37   John 4:34   John 12:26

You are entering a great harvest that you did not labor for.
All I ask is that you willingly lay aside your own pursuits to follow Mine, and in doing so, I will fulfill the desires of your heart.
Your life will be renewed as you walk in obedience to what I ask.
Enjoy the journey and declare aloud, "Your will be done on earth as it is in heaven."
I will drop handfuls on purpose for you as you move through the fields I have prepared—ready and waiting for the harvest.
You will be filled with joy as you partake of this work with Me.
See, I have called you by name for this great harvest of souls.
Look with Me at what I have placed in your hands and be about your Father's business.
Blessed are those in whom I have confidence, who respond to My beckoning.
When I return, you will receive your reward and rule with Me in glory.

November 29

Liberty

Stand fast therefore in the liberty by which Christ has made us free, and do not be entangled again with a yoke of bondage.
—*Galatians 5:1 (NKJV)*

See also: Galatians 5:2-13

You will find freedom where the flame of your love ignites your passion for all that I Am.
Freedom is the wind beneath your soul, lifting you to new heights in My presence.
Listen to the call of My Spirit, and let freedom become your battle cry.
Let My freedom reign in every part of your life, for where My Spirit is, there is liberty.
You were created to live free from everything that separates us.
Remain unchained and unafraid until I return.

November 30

Obedience

Search me, O God, and know my heart, try me, and know my anxieties, and see if there is any wicked way in me, and lead me in the way everlasting.
—*Psalm 139:23–24 (NKJV)*

See also: Romans 6:16   Galatians 6:4   1 John 1:9

Be obedient in the small things, for they prepare you for greater trust.
Be willing to look deeply into your own heart and come into the light of My examination.
Do not hide in the crevices of darkness where fear dwells.
Confess your weaknesses and faults often, for humility keeps your heart soft before Me.
Be vulnerable with Me, not with the world, for in your openness, I will shape you into purity and strength.

All That I Am

December

December 1

A Life of Love

Now hope does not disappoint, because the love of God has been poured out in our hearts by the Holy Spirit who was given to us.
— *Romans 5:5 (NKJV)*

See also: Psalm 118:4   Song of Songs 3:11   Song of Songs 6:3

Who truly knows My great love?
It is known by those who have heard the wedding bells of heaven and run into My waiting arms.
Let love arise within you and overflow to others who have answered the call of divine affection.
You are irrevocably Mine—sealed in covenant and carried in My embrace.
From this high place of refuge, begin to live anew with Me.
Your dreams are woven into Mine, for My greatest desire is *us—together.*

December 2

Peace on Earth

For unto us a Child is born,
Unto us a Son is given;
And the government will be upon His shoulder.
And His name will be called
Wonderful, Counselor, Mighty God,
Everlasting Father, Prince of Peace.
—Isaiah 9:6 (NKJV)

See also: Ezekiel 37:26   Luke 2:14   John 14:27

You have nothing to fear, for you are safe within My peace.
My peace will guard your mind like a fortress, shielding you from the enemy's attacks.
It will calm your body and fill you with life.
Peace is always a choice—choose it in every situation.
You will know My peace when chaos surrounds you, yet your heart remains still.
That calm is Me, for I Am there in your midst.
Be content in this truth, for it will sustain you through the difficult days ahead.
I Am Peace, and I dwell within you.

December 3

God Became Us

Therefore the Lord Himself will give you a sign: Behold, the virgin shall conceive and bear a Son, and shall call His name Immanuel.
—*Isaiah 7:14 (NKJV)*

See also: Matthew 1:23   John 1:14

I became one of you, bringing gifts from heaven—Love, Peace, Joy, and Forgiveness.
I came to light the way back to the Father of Lights, that you might walk in the radiance of His glory.
Now I ask, who will go in faith to do the impossible with Me?
You are called to believe when others doubt.
Say to My people, "The Lord is with us!"

December 4

These Days

> Then he said, 'Take the arrows', so he took them. And he said to the king of Israel, 'Strike the ground', so he struck three times and stopped. And the man of God was angry with him and said, 'You should have struck five or six times, then you would have struck Syria till you had destroyed it, but now you will strike Syria only three times.'
> —2 Kings 13:18-19 (NKJV)

The time is now to rise like Elisha, performing great wonders in My Name so that all may know there is a God who is mighty and shows Himself strong on behalf of His people.

My Spirit has fallen and will continue to fall upon those of My choosing—those who will give an answer to a questioning world that asks, "Is there a God who can be inquired of?"

I will pour out My Spirit without measure upon all who believe Me—for healing, for heavenly vision, for provision, and for raising the dead in My Name.

Strike the arrows of your faith with boldness, believing Me for greater victories.

The measure of your faith will determine the measure of your triumph.

These are the days of My power—walk in them!

December 5

The Judge

I, the Lord, search the heart,
I test the mind,
Even to give every man according to his ways,
According to the fruit of his doings.
— *Jeremiah 17:10 (NKJV)*

See also: Matthew 7:1   Romans 14:4   James 4:11-12

Give up all judgment and you will be free to see both Me and others rightly. Say to Me, "Lord, give me eyes to see as You see, and give me Your heart as well." I desire you, My child, to remain innocent of presumptuous sins. Keep your heart pure before Me, and let Me be the Judge, for I alone know the hearts of men.

How can others see you clearly if you hide behind judgment as your defense? As you release your right to judge, I will restore your true identity and teach you to walk in acceptance and love toward all whom I place before you.

December 6

Into the Deep

And He said to them,
Cast the net on the right side of the boat, and you will find some.
So they cast, and now they were not able to draw it in
because of the multitude of fish.
— *John 21:6 (NKJV)*

See also: Philippians 2:3   1 Thessalonians 5:13

Go ahead, cast out into the deep, knowing that I Am for you. I Am bringing others beside you—those who will influence you, spur you on, and open many doors. Some will bring honesty and humility; others will cheer you forward. Esteem them and recognize what I Am doing in your midst. Now go, and step boldly into uncharted waters with Me.

December 7

The Way of the Lord

And one shall say, Heap it up, heap it up, prepare the way, take the stumbling block out of the way of My people.
—Isaiah 57:14 (NKJV)

Come, prepare the way of the Lord, for I stand at the door of time, awaiting a triumphal entry.
Now is the day to go out in great joy,
proclaiming My goodness, graciousness, and mercy.
Do not say these days are dark or evil,
for I declare they are days of harvest and My fields are ready!
Take up the sickle in your hand,
for the immediate harvest is My great love.
Call all to Me from the compassion of My heart, and they will come.
Say to them, "The time of restoration has come—come and be restored!"

December 8

The Bigger Picture

**For You have armed me with strength for the battle;
You have subdued under me those who rose up against me.**
— *Psalm 18:39 (NKJV)*

See also: Ephesians 3:16-19   Jude 1:21

You are a stranger in a foreign land, for you belong to Me.
Look from above and see the bigger picture.
Your assignment on earth is to discern the battle between good and evil.
Be strong and courageous—this is My command!
The time has come to take your place beside Me in My Kingdom.
Let living with Me become your greatest satisfaction.
Eternity is approaching,
and time is rushing in!

December 9

The Protection of God

> For He put on righteousness as a breastplate,
> And a helmet of salvation on His head;
> He put on the garments of vengeance for clothing,
> And was clad with zeal as a cloak.
> —*Isaiah 59:17 (NKJV)*

See also: Jeremiah 46:3-4   Ephesians 6:11-12

Have I not provided you with all the protection you need? Let My covering keep your mind in perfect peace. Your heart is a target, vulnerable to the darts of the evil one, so clothe yourself in My righteousness. The core of your being was made for Me; let My truth uphold the very center of who you are.
Now lift up faith—faith that believes My words and acts upon them. Take hold of My spoken word, for it carries the power to accomplish My will in your life. My armor will cause you to stand in peace and live each day in victory.

December 10

Immanuel

"Behold, the virgin shall be with child, and bear a Son, and they shall call His name Immanuel," which is translated, "God with us."
— *Matthew 1:23 (NKJV)*

See also: Isaiah 7:14

Immanuel is My union with your nature, announced from the beginning as the promise of My coming to dwell with you. I came to be united with you in your humanity. Call Me Immanuel, and you will know My presence.
Let My Name become a living reality within you, saying, "Immanuel—my God is with me!" Sense My nearness surrounding and sustaining you. I Am Immanuel. Claim this Name, and allow it to shape the very essence of who you are in Me.

December 11

God's Evidence

> Now then, stand here, because I am going to confront you with evidence before the Lord as to all the righteous acts performed by the Lord for you and your ancestors.
> —1 Samuel 12:7 (NKJV)

See also: Psalm 46:10

Stand quietly before Me, your Lord, as I remind you of the great things I have done for you—the gifts I have given, the things I have restored that were once lost or stolen.

I Am the One who brought the connection you so deeply needed, the grace and influence beyond what you expected.

I Am the Repairer of relationships, of family, of friendships, and of the wounds from your past.

Look for the evidence of My love, for My love is being made real to you—and there is more to come.

In quietness and stillness you will be established as you reflect on the wonderful things I have done for you this year.

December 12

That Day

> And Jesus cried out with a loud voice, and breathed His last. Then the veil of the temple was torn in two from top to bottom.
> —*Mark 15:37-38 (NKJV)*

See also: Luke 24:5   John 19:38-42

Friday: That Day
The wind rose in violence, and darkness covered the land.
The earth trembled as God's blood was poured out.
The veil in the temple was torn in two; the graves gave up their dead.
The tears of the faithful could not be contained.
The mother of Jesus was stricken with agony, witnessing the violent death of The Promise.

Saturday: That Day
The earth lay silent, the sun dimmed in mourning.
Hope seemed lost among the living; it could not be found.
Behind closed doors came the sound of weeping.
Fear and confusion pressed upon My children as the enemy laughed in mockery.
The words of Jesus felt like a dream—fading before they could take root.

Sunday: That Day
The morning sun rose and stood bright as noon.
A shout of joy moved through the earth.
Angels descended to the tomb, and grief was overturned.
Burial balm became anointing oil as it fell to the ground.
Death was defeated, and victory was proclaimed in the upper room, as three women sent two men running to see the proof—that life and triumph are found in You!

December 13

Bringing the Kingdom

And when they had come into the house, they saw the young Child with Mary His mother, and fell down and worshiped Him. And when they had opened their treasures, they presented gifts to Him: gold, frankincense, and myrrh.
—*Matthew 2:11 (NKJV)*

See also: Luke 2:14   Luke 2:20

There is a Kingdom revealed, traveled to on roads of old.
Follow the star into the field—tell the Story.
You carry the treasures of heaven to earth, riding on camels laden with gold.
Bring the tidings of My peace on earth, of My love and glory,
the news of a new birth that changes all things.
Go—do not remain!
Be bold, and take My gifts wherever you go.

December 14

My Peace

I will hear what God the Lord will speak, For He will speak peace To His people and to His saints; But let them not turn back to folly.
—*Psalm 85:8 (NKJV)*

See also: John 14:27

My peace is a river flowing down from the throne room of God.
I Am there in that peace, for My Name is the Prince of Peace.
My peace surpasses circumstances and time, for it is eternal, and I never withdraw this gift. The peace of this world is only a fleeting imitation of what I give you.
My peace is priceless—abiding, unshakable, and yours to keep.

December 15

Faith Is...

While we do not look at the things which are seen, but at the things which are not seen, for the things which are seen are temporary, but the things which are not seen are eternal.
– 2 Corinthians 4:18 (NKJV)

See also: Hebrews 11:1-10

Faith is trust placed fully and confidently in My hands.
Faith is stepping into the unknown when nothing around you feels certain.
Faith is doing what looks impossible simply because I asked.
Faith is choosing My reward instead of the praise of people.
Faith is seeing with My eyes when your own sight fails you.
Faith is dropping every distraction and every burden so you can run toward all that I Am without hesitation.
Faith is the courage that turns obedience into victory, and the path where you discover who you truly are in Me.

December 16

The Glory

And there I will meet with the children of Israel, and the tabernacle shall be sanctified by My glory.
—*Exodus 29:43 (NKJV)*

See also: Jeremiah 23:23   Ephesians 2:13   2 Corinthians 3:18

In stillness, My presence is made known.
Holiness surrounds the place where I Am near.
In My glory, your heart grows quiet, and time fades away.
Here, you and I are undone—worship flows in these sacred moments.
Be still… and become One with Me.

December 17

Finish Well

But none of these things move me; nor do I count my life dear to myself, so that I may finish my race with joy, and the ministry which I received from the Lord Jesus, to testify to the gospel of the grace of God.
—*Acts 20:24 (NKJV)*

See also: Colossians 3:17   James 1:4

Live in the expectancy of My appearing, finishing the course I have set before you.
Do all things for the glory of My Name, for I Am your sure reward.
I will be to you a Father, a Brother, and a Friend as you cross the finish line—finishing well to the very end!

December 18

Apprehending Truth

Listen to counsel and receive instruction, That you may be wise in your latter days.
—*Proverbs 19:20 (NKJV)*

See also: Ecclesiastes 7:25   Proverbs 8:1-11

Let your confidence rest in Me as you seek My understanding rather than more knowledge. Remind your soul to pursue My wisdom, for I long to be your Teacher.
I alone keep you from error, giving you the right words at the right time.
I Am the sound judgment your heart desires.
I alone can guard you from pride, false humility, and wrong judgment, for I give you My thoughts as you open your heart to receive.
I Am the longing within you to walk in truth.
Treasure what I alone can give, and listen for My voice each day.

December 19

Look

> This was the Lord's doing;
> It is marvelous in our eyes.
> This is the day the Lord has made;
> We will rejoice and be glad in it.
> — *Psalm 118:23–24 (NKJV)*

See also: Psalm 95:7   Matthew 6:34   Luke 11:3

Look to Me for everything, and know that each day is a new beginning.
Anticipate what I Am about to do in your life today, for I never take My eyes off you.
Trust that I Am already ahead of you, preparing the way.
Nothing escapes My sight, and nothing can hinder My plans for you.
Walk with expectation, for My goodness is waiting for you every day.

December 20

The Gates

Enter into His gates with thanksgiving, And into His courts with praise. Be thankful to Him, and bless His name.
—Psalm 100:4 (NKJV)

See also: Isaiah 26:2   Matthew 7:13   John 10:7-9

At the Gate Beautiful, My power to heal was made known—for there I Am revealed as the Lord who heals.
At the Sheepfold Gate, you enter into My rest, spending time with Me beside the still waters that flow into the River of Life.
At the Narrow Gate, you enter into My approval, where I anoint you with the oil of gladness.
At the Gate of Thanksgiving, you find the entrance into My praise.
At the Heavenly Gate, My glory is unveiled, and you are welcomed to sit with Me in My throne room.
I paid for entry into these gates with the price of My blood,
that you might know Me in every way.

December 21

Battle Ready

Put on the whole armor of God, that you may be able to stand against the wiles of the devil.
—*Ephesians 6:11 (NKJV)*

See also: Ephesians 6:10–18

I have often wondered about the armor of God.
Today I declare that I am blessed.
I am a new creation, covered in Christ.
I will walk in the truth that sets me free from condemnation.
I live in His Kingdom—free and full of love.
I am a daughter of God, filled with power and purpose.
I will succeed in the plans God has for me.
I am an overcomer, walking in the victory Christ has won. In the Name of Jesus, I take hold of all that is mine.
I live in the peace that crushes Satan beneath my feet.
God is my health, my wisdom, and my life.
I will change the world for His glory and fame.
I will stand in unshakable faith, never denying who He says I am.
I will fulfill all He has entrusted to me.
This is my armor today—I put it on.

December 22

Desperate

And you will seek Me and find *Me*, when you search for Me with all your heart.
—*Jeremiah 29:13 (NKJV)*

See also: Psalm 119:24   Hebrews 8:10-11

Give to Me this space of authority I long for—a place where you can be My playful child who knows that I Am good. Talk with Me, and then listen for My response.
Put away your own ways of searching, for I desire to give you new insight and a deeper revelation of Myself that goes beyond understanding. Acknowledge where you have sought Me only on the surface, and come now with holy desperation.
I Am looking for the wonder in your prayer and the awe in your worship—for there, you will find Me waiting.

December 23

Heaven Comes Down

*And they asked Baruch, saying, Tell us now,
how did you write all these words at his instruction.
So Baruch answered them, He proclaimed with his mouth all these
words to me, and I wrote them with ink in the book.*
—*Jeremiah 36:17-18 (NKJV)*

See also: Jeremiah 30:2   Habakkuk 2:2   Matthew 25:15-28

When you create with Me, we step into a holy collaboration that brings heaven into the sightline of earth. There is a quiet place where I have given you eyes to see into My realm. From that place, you help lift the veil so others can know and perceive what they could not on their own.

You are called to take what you see in heaven and reveal it through words, through color, through movement, so others may behold who I Am. What I allow you to see and carry becomes the doorway through which the unseen enters the world.

Give freely the talents I have placed in your hands, so that I may receive My reward.

Paint with Me. Write with Me. Worship and dance with Me.

December 24

Victorious

But thanks be to God, who gives us the victory through our Lord Jesus Christ. Therefore, my beloved brethren, be steadfast, immovable, always abounding in the work of the Lord, knowing that your labor is not in vain in the Lord.
—*1 Corinthians 15:57-58 (NKJV)*

See also: 1 John 5:4-5   Romans 8:37

I have created you to win every battle—both spiritual and physical.
What you accomplish in this world mirrors what is taking place in the spirit.
Press on, and you will prevail.
It is the soul at rest that finds its victories.
For when you fight from peace, you fight from My strength.
Do not measure your success by what you see, but by your obedience to Me—for every act of faith released is another's victory.

December 25

Give

**The generous soul will be made rich,
And he who waters will also be watered himself.**
— *Proverbs 11:25 (NKJV)*

See also: Luke 6:30-38   2 Corinthians 9:7-12

Pour out what I have placed within you, and you will make room for more. Have I not said you will receive in greater measure—pressed down, shaken together, and running over?

As I fill your cup, look for opportunities to pour into others.

Give from your own storehouse, and you will become a vessel of overflow—a cup, even a well, of refreshment to those around you.

Remember, the flow continues only when you give from what you have been given.

December 26

Today

If then God so clothes the grass, which today is in the field and tomorrow is thrown into the oven, how much more will He clothe you, O you of little faith?
—Luke 12:28 (NKJV)

See also: Hebrews 13:8

Today, I will walk on water—confident in Christ my Savior, rejoicing in faith.
Today, I will expect His goodness and see Jesus in everything.
Today, and every day, I will live in the wonder of His presence.

December 27

Glory Days

So it shall be, while My glory passes by, that I will put you in the cleft of the rock, and will cover you with My hand while I pass by.
—*Exodus 33:22 (NKJV)*

See also: Psalm 3:3   Ephesians 3:3-13   Revelation 2:17

You will grow stronger as you seek My glory.
I will provide you with hidden manna to sustain you each day.
In times of trial and testing, I will come to you with My power to strengthen and uphold you.
I Am your shield and your fortress in these days of glory.

December 28

By My Side

For I am jealous for you with godly jealousy. For I have betrothed you to one husband, that I may present you as a chaste virgin to Christ.
— *2 Corinthians 11:2 (NKJV)*

See also: Genesis 2:19   John 19:34   2 Corinthians 11:2

As I took Eve from Adam's side, making her his equal in position, so I have brought you forth from My Son's side to be My Bride.
This is your royal position—by My side.
I have called you My friend and My child, but now I call you Bride.
Learn what it means to sit and reign with Me, side by side in My Kingdom.

December 29

Understanding God

**For you did not receive the spirit of bondage again to fear,
but you received the Spirit of adoption by whom we cry out,
Abba, Father.**
— *Romans 8:15 (NKJV)*

See also: John 15:26   John 16:13-15   1 Corinthians 2:7-16

Understand that I Am not a withholding God.
What I have written, I have done—and I will do again, for I Am eternal.
My promises are both now and coming to you in fullness.
My Spirit searches the depths of all that is Mine, even the secret counsels of My heart, to reveal them to you.

I long to lift you to new heights of faith, where you are taught and led by My Spirit.

December 30

Confidence

In the fear of the Lord there is strong confidence, And His children will have a place of refuge.
—*Proverbs 14:26 (NKJV)*

See also: Ephesians 3:12   Hebrews 10:35-36   1 John 3:21

Be confident in Me, for I Am your God who hears and answers you.
Only believe and trust in Me, for I Am able to deliver you.
I Am your Confidence and your unfailing strength.
Do not let uncertainty move you, for I have gone before you.
My faithfulness surrounds you like a shield, and My Word will not fail.
Stand firm in this truth—I Am with you, and I will not disappoint those who trust in Me.

December 31

A God Quote

But I say to you, love your enemies, bless those who curse you, do good to those who hate you, and pray for those who spitefully use you and persecute you.
—*Matthew 5:44 (NKJV)*

See also: Song of Songs 8:6   Luke 6:28-35   John 15:9

LOVE IS:
The most powerful force in the universe—it conquers fear, heals wounds, and never fails.
It is the breath of the Holy Spirit flowing through every act of grace, awakening hearts to the very heartbeat of God.

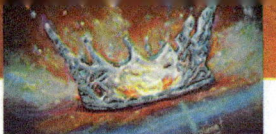

Closing

As you reach the end of this devotional, my prayer is that something within you has awakened. Not to more information, but to relationship. Not simply to Scriptures on a page, but to the living God who speaks, heals, restores, and walks beside you in every unseen moment.

My journey has been one of valleys and altars, laughter and tears, trials that felt unbearable, and miracles that could only come from the Father who calls each of us by name. Every page you have read was born out of conversations with Him, and it is my hope that these conversations have stirred your own.

The God who met me as a little girl on the way to school, who carried me through years of brokenness, who healed my body and uncovered my heart, is the same God who is pursuing you now. He has been writing the story of your life long before you ever held this book. Nothing in your past has disqualified you from His presence, His love, or His calling. He desires your heart, your trust, and your friendship.

If there is one truth that I pray remains with you, it is this: you are deeply known, deeply loved, and continually invited into the knowledge of the Holy One. This knowing is not a one-time revelation. It is the ongoing discovery of His character, His voice, and His nearness as you walk with Him day by day. Your history with God is still unfolding, and every time He moves in your life, your understanding of Him grows richer and more real.

So as you close this book, do not close the door to the journey. Keep asking. Keep listening. Keep noticing the ways He is revealing Himself in the ordinary and the extraordinary. Open your heart to the surprises He has prepared for you, for He delights to be found by those who seek Him.

May the God who healed me, restored me, and called me to paint and write, do the same and more in you. May His presence fill your days, may His love steady your steps, and may His voice become the sweetest sound you know.

This is not the end. It is another beginning. Walk forward with expectation. Your Healer, your Father, and your closest Friend is with you.

All that I am, and all that you are becoming, rests in Him.

—Dianne Tylski

About the Author

Dianne is a California native whose love for art began early, sketching in her grade school classrooms. In high school she continued developing her craft through a mail-in art program, and her teacher later entered her into a competition to redesign the city seal of Escondido. She won, earning a year of published artwork and a scholarship to Biola Bible College.

In her fifties, Dianne combined her artistic skill with her husband's photography to create one-of-a-kind bridal albums, each designed as a personal keepsake.

Everything shifted in 2013 when Dianne attended Bethel Church in Redding and was healed of melanoma. That encounter awakened a new sensitivity to God's presence. As she listened to worship music, she began seeing vivid images in her mind's eye and hearing phrases that carried weight. These impressions became the seeds of both her artwork and her writing.

Out of that experience she launched "Art That Speaks," a ministry devoted to prophetic creativity. Today, Dianne focuses on creating art that carries the messages she senses from heaven, and she teaches others to use their God given gifts to reach the world with hope and truth.

You can order a print of any of my paintings on art paper or canvas by contacting me directly by Facebook Messenger or by email tylskidianne@gmail.com.

See more of my paintings at Diannetylski.com or visit my Facebook page, Christian Writers Guild.